Achtung Architektur!

Graham Foundation/MIT Press Series in Contemporary Architectural Discourse

Achtung Architektur! Image and Phantasm in Contemporary Austrian Architecture, by Eeva-Liisa Pelkonen

Graham Foundation for Advanced Studies in the Fine Arts

Chicago, Illinois

Eeva-Liisa Pelkonen

Achtung

Image and Phantasm

in Contemporary Austrian Architecture

Architektur!

The MIT Press

Cambridge, Massachusetts

London, England

For my parents

 Publication of this book has been supported by a grant from the Graham Foundation for Advanced Studies in the Fine Arts.

This book was set in Joanna by Graphic Composition, Inc.
Printed on recycled paper and bound in the United States of America.

Library of Congress Cataloging-in-Publication Data

Pelkonen, Eeva-Liisa.
    Achtung Architektur! : image and phantasm in contemporary Austrian architecture / Eeva-Liisa Pelkonen.
        p.   cm.
    In English.
    Includes bibliographical references and index.
    ISBN 0-262-16159-1 (hc : alk. paper)
    1. Architecture—Austria—Graz.   2. Architecture, Modern—20th century—Austria—Graz.   I. Title.
    NA1010.G7P45   1996
    720'.9436'5—dc20   96-10497
                                                                              CIP

Contents

Preface

This project is about a way of *thinking architecture*, not to be confused with thinking *about* architecture, which is always marked by a certain distance. The late Finnish architect Reima Pietilä spoke poignantly about "the smell of architecture." I would like this book to mediate that "smell"—a kind of intimacy with architecture. This way of *thinking architecture* corresponds with a similar way of *making architecture* that allows almost any image, concept, or thing to have its architectural translation. I have in mind a kind of child's way of looking at the world, being able to transform one thing into another and to imagine something that does not yet exist. This unfettered vision allows that everything can serve as a beginning for architecture, everything is possible! It is exactly this notion of transporting ideas and images into architecture (and the other way round), which denies a closure of architectural discourse, that this book is about.

I am most indebted to Volker Giencke, for it was particularly his works and our discussions that triggered the will to write this book. In Giencke's office, where I worked between 1988 and 1992, we all shared this will to *play* with architecture. I am grateful for having had the opportunity to profit from the architectural climate I shared with Nives Anicic, Fredl Bramberger, Arthur van der Broek, Robert Clerici, Arpad Ferdinand, Davide Ferrero, Wolfgang Feyferlik, Susi Fritzer, Uta Giencke, Erwin Matzer, Claudius Pratsch, Robert Vucic, and others. I also thank Luzie Giencke for searching the archives at Giencke & Co. for images to be published in this book.

I am grateful to the organizations and individuals who helped me in this project. First, I want to thank *Bundesministerium für Wissenschaft und Forschung* (Austrian Ministry for Science and Research) for their generous grant, which made this project possible. My special thanks go to Dr. Elisabeth Wiesbauer-Menasse for believing in it from the very beginning. I am also grateful to Dr. Hofrat Wolfdieter Dreibholz for his support, and to Karl Fitzthum and Lotte Pöchacker for their editorial help and advice when I was preparing the study proposal. I also thank the Finland–United States Educational Exchange Service and the Fulbright Commission for enabling my studies at Yale School of Architecture in 1992–1993.

The actual writing process would have been impossible without the generous help of Professor Karsten Harries from the Department of Philosophy at Yale University during 1992 to 1994, when I participated in the advanced program in architectural theory at the Yale School of Architecture. He helped me to understand the Austrian and German culture, from Nietzsche to Sedlmayr and Heidegger, and most of all to find my way of *writing architecture*. Also at the Yale School of Architecture, I thank Margot Villecco for her help and for paying such careful attention to language, and Alan Plattus for reading and commenting on the work, and Kent Bloomer for leading me to the insights of ornaments.

Comments made by Roger Connah, Kenneth Frampton, Michael Hays, and Joan Ockman helped me to revise the manuscript. At The MIT Press I thank Roger Conover for his enthusiasm in the project, Sandra Minkkinen for her careful editing and production assistance, and Jean Wilcox for designing the book. I am grateful for the grant from the Graham Foundation for Advanced Studies in the Fine Arts, which helped me to prepare the book for publishing. I also thank Ernie Brooks for his editorial comments.

I have been supported and encouraged in many ways by good friends and colleagues in Finland, Austria, and the United States. In Finland I thank Roger Connah, Meri Mäkipentti, and Antti Veltheim with whom I have shared most of the very early ideas about architecture. At Yale my gratitude goes to my colleagues at the Masters of Environmental Design program—Thomas Forget, David Haney, Raleigh Perkins, and Peter Soland—and to Lance Duerfahrd from the Department of Comparative Literature for discussions and friendship.

While writing this book I have often reflected upon the personal experiences and conversations I had with friends and colleagues in Graz and in Vienna. It is impossible to name everybody in this context, but I want to thank them all for giving me insight into the Austrian culture. As a foreigner I hope to be excused for my shortcomings; I often found myself bewildered by a culture where eccentricity is part of the tradition. I also want to thank Susanna Ahvonen and Markus Pernthaler in Graz, and Uta Giencke, Walter Buck, and Pekka Janhunen in Vienna for offering me their hospitality during my visits to Austria.

Finally, my very special thanks go to Turner Brooks for sharing the excitement that accompanies the publication of any first book.

Achtung
Architektur!

Introduction

As the title *Achtung Architektur!* suggests, this book discusses architecture that entails a surprise, even danger. Shock is introduced as a limit condition for contemporary architecture; architectural work is here understood as a machine for producing certain effects that challenge the perceiving and experiencing subject. My approach pursues this psychic dimension in which experience is considered something interactive and responsive, pertaining to the imagination and to the imaginary. In this sense the title also implies that the book focuses on how architecture works rather than what it means.[1] My approach is critical of the traditional predominantly visual and contemplative understanding of architectural perception. The notion of experience leads to a reconsideration of the role of the subject in the perception process: the subject reduced to a mobile eye yields to an anticipating and desiring subject with an active emotional investment in the environment.

Three goals are relevant for my endeavor: first, to reassess how contemporary European architecture pertains to the modern tradition; second, to examine the relationship between architecture and the particular intellectual, cultural, political, and social status of postwar Europe; and, third, to discuss how local cultural politics and art in the postwar period can be used as keys to understanding recent developments in Austrian architecture.

Michel Foucault summarizes the intellectual climate of postwar Europe as follows: "During the years 1945–1965 (I am referring to Europe), there was a certain way of thinking correctly, a certain style of political discourse, a certain aesthetics of the intellectual. One had to be on familiar terms with Marx, not let one's dream stray too far from Freud." In addition, the era was dominated by "an amalgam of revolutionary and anti-repressive politics."[2] This book traces the connection between the general postwar intellectual culture dominated by this Marxist-Freudian twist and what has become a very particular architectural climate in today's Austria.

I maintain that the most radical Austrian architecture after the 1960s tried to reassess the modern tradition in general and that of the avant-garde in particular by redefining the architectural experience that stems from this Marxist-Freudian emphasis.[3] According to this strategy, art and architecture became the ultimate desire machines, producing effects that tell us what could be rather than what already is, reflecting both subjective and collective wish-thinking. They thus express what Ernst Bloch called "the Utopian impulse,"[4] a gesture toward something "not-yet-present" (Bloch), and thus prepare for transformation and change.

The projects I have chosen for closer scrutiny all share the central concern of contemporary Marxist cultural theory of how images can enter the realm of the active imagination that prompts such an impulse. My approach can be considered psychoanalytic in that I believe that architecture can free desire, and philosophical in that concepts respond to images. The correspondence between writing and making architecture can be found exactly in this realm of active imagination and memory that helps us trace how the real is drawn into the realm of thought.

The main question I try to address is therefore, how does one introduce desire into architecture?[5] Thinkers such as Henri Lefebvre and Fredric Jameson are important. Following Lefebvre, I will show that to constitute desire, space can simultaneously "assert, negate and deny."[6] A central concern is to discuss architecture not as a thing-in-itself, but as a fictive reality: "Reality of the object, insofar as it is produced by desire," writes Foucault, "is thus a *psychic reality*."[7] Following Jameson, I have emphasized the act of interpretation; the subject participates in the construction of reality, its myths as well as its transformation. I agree with Jameson that this new cultural production should invite such numerous readings, that is, new realities. The constitution of desire enhances this potential.

The redefinition of experience addresses the question of how architecture triggers the fictional readings through which it enters the realm of poetics and active imagination. Instead of reification, shock and surprise produce what Roland Barthes calls "a poetic or semantic 'accident.'"[8] Throughout my study I concentrated on such moments of rupture and accidents—*Achtung!*—through which a work reveals its emotional content and the impulse toward a certain disposition. These ruptures are key for understanding how architecture can awaken active imagination and, perhaps, on a more permanent basis, transform consciousness. Chapter 1, "Architecture as an Event," discusses how such ruptures are effected. The work under discussion, the Red Stage, is emblematic of my whole endeavor.

Although it accepts the validity of the modern project, the work I discuss shuns simple fascination with modernist and avant-garde revolutions alike. This book tries to locate this work through the concept of the peripheral by discussing tendencies within twentieth-century architecture that test the limits of the modern tradition. Peripheral architecture challenges the traditional paradigms of objecthood, compositional form, programmatic functionality, and spatial closure. Taking contemporary European, particularly Austrian, architecture as a focus, my thesis traces the strategies of such peripheral work by discussing projects that introduce new themes into the discourse: temporality, phantasm, happening, and gesturality. These moves all trigger the imagination through their own poetics: thickness of meaning, symbolic coding, and ambiguity. While tracing the main paradigms (obsessions!) of the work under scrutiny, my main goal is to establish how this contemporary architecture rewrites the modern tradition through transgression, reversal, and negation, all of which question the traditional modes of representation.

In the second chapter, "Peripheral Notions," I discuss the following architectural paradigms that are relevant to contemporary Austrian architecture and that demonstrate what I call a peripheral relationship to the modern tradition: the *organic*, as a means of both questioning formal abstraction as a basic category of canonical modernism and of (re)introducing aperspectival space into architecture; the *Großraum* as questioning the idea of programmatic space and introducing notions of play and festival; blurring of the relationship between *architecture and landscape*, where nature is no longer understood as a mere container, but also as a thing contained within architecture; and *glass architecture* as a means of introducing hallucinatory, phantastic character. Playing with fluctuating moments of revealing and concealing, seeing and nonseeing, glass architecture is a domain of architecture that occupies the threshold where dream and reality begin to blur, making it perhaps the ultimate phantasm in the tradition of modern architecture. All of the works presented here return to these paradigms, which constitute perhaps the most ambiguous side of the modern tradition. The third chapter, "Toward the Aesthetics of the Incomplete," considers how materiality, texture, and structure can further challenge the functional and formal.

The last chapter, "The New Avant-Garde?", returns to the Austrian condition—to its redefinition of avant-garde and the influence of such tendencies as *art informel*, tachism, and happening art on architectural discourse. Phenomenology and existentialism as well as Marxist art and cultural criticism contribute to a redefinition of the function of art and to what I argue is a characteristically Austrian understanding of the idea of engaged architecture.

Against the political background of Austrian postwar art and architecture, the word *Achtung* (beware!) implies the political challenge they offer when they come to be understood as something that potentially has the ability to transform our relationship with the world as well as our understanding of reality. The politics of architecture are here based on the belief that architecture, by its very nature, has the capacity to engage people in an interaction with the world and even transform the real.

Most important for this reassessment of experience as it pertains to the politics of contemporary architecture is the dislocation of the subject. As Giorgio Agamben states, "unconscious experience is not a subjective experience"[9] but something that connects with the collective and the communal.[10] The shift from the subjective spatiotemporal experience toward a more active and engaged relationship with the environment enhances this view of the collective; unlike the abstracted coolness of canonical modernism and the aesthetizing tendencies of the early avant-gardes, what has been referred to as engaged architecture can be understood as the move from the subjective "psycho-poetics" of experience toward the search for the communal. Perhaps the most ambitious goal of my project, therefore, is to relocate the ethical by finding gestures that suggest the communal and the political in contemporary architecture.

In keeping with the initial premise—architecture understood as something that works, that has an operative function—it is possible to conclude that the body of works I have chosen for discussion shuns closure both in a literal as well as a phenomenal sense; architecture can hardly be considered as a complete thing-in-itself, it must be seen as something incomplete, temporal, and fragmentary, gesturing toward something.

I would like to borrow Barthes's concept of *écriture* to characterize this condition: *écriture* implies that architecture is understood as a "a field of action, the definition of, and hope for, a possibility."[11]

Within every literary form, there is a general choice of tone, of ethos, if you like, and this is precisely where the writer shows himself clearly as an individual because this is where he commits himself. A language and a style are data prior to all problematics of language, they are the natural product of Time and of the person as a biological entity; but the formal identity of the writer is truly established only outside the permanence of grammatical norms and stylistic constants, where the written continuum, first collected and enclosed within a perfectly innocent linguistic nature, at last becomes a total sign, the choice of a human attitude, the affirmation of certain Good.[12]

Through the works discussed I want to locate the space for this ethos in architecture through the notion of the peripheral. Rather than aiming to define the state of things, for example, by analyzing form and different organizational principles, my interest is in locating the dimension that talks about the sense of architecture in general and the disposition of individual works in particular. Whether referring to a geographical location, to the relationship with modern tradition, or to minor peripheral names, periphery and peripheral imply the possibility of taking architecture beyond questions of form and language. I believe that they have recently made the modern tradition come alive: the search for the eternal state of things and the attempt to fix language has finally been overthrown by the rediscovery of the potential within the modern to encompass a certain ethical dimension and a certain freedom that can exist only outside language.

I have concentrated my discussion on a very limited number of examples. I chose Graz, the capital of Styria, a province in western Austria, because I happen to be familiar with its architectural culture. Such a geographically peripheral place lacks the metropolitan exaggeration and too-easy transports of ideas typical of the centers. Precisely for that reason it offers more subtle ways to reassess the modern tradition while being simultaneously responsive to recent international debates and trends.

In the catalog *Architektur aus Graz* from 1981, one finds the first critical treatment of this development. Friedrich Achleitner writes in his introduction as follows: "The break in the 60s had definite consequences. Graz reacted faster, stronger and without preconception (less critically?) towards international tendencies. Whereas in Wien even the slogan 'Everything is architecture' recalled historical universalism, the counter position of Graz preferred its own interpretations of architectural traditions." [13] Although participating in and echoing the same international trends within architecture and urbanism as its counterpart, Vienna, Graz was soon to acquire an identity all its own, filtering ideas through inventive and unorthodox use of materials and structure, and shamelessly mixing different elements in the modern tradition, such as high-tech and the organic. Maybe the most provocative manifestation of the attitudes developing in Graz during the late 1960s onward is Günther Domenig's Zentralsparkasse building in the Favoriten district in Vienna, completed in 1979, which managed to shock with its voluptuous animosity.

By that time Graz was already known for its cultural experiments not only in the field of architecture, but also in literature—Peter Handke, Ingeborg Bachman, Wolfgang Bauer, and Barbara Frischmuth being the leading figures—and for its famous jazz academy. The desire to establish a cultural identity independent of the Viennese hegemony culminated in 1968 when the first international avant-garde festival called *steirischer herbst* ("Styrian autumn") took place. Now an established annual event, *steirischer herbst* has strong emphasis on contemporary music, experimental films, theatre, art, and architecture. It is famous for performing the early Handke plays, for staging the first Thomas Bernhard play ever to be performed in Austria, and for functioning as a showcase for several young artists during its twenty years of existence. Two parallel events take place annually: *Steirische Akademie* (Styrian Academy), an international symposium focusing on contemporary issues, and *Trigon-biennale*, founded in 1963, which shows art from three neighboring countries, Austria, Italy, and the former Yugoslavia. The former talks about the active desire to belong in the world culture, and the latter manifests the desire of Graz to disassociate itself even geographically from Vienna. One can sense this militancy toward Vienna, still dominant among the members of the *Grazer Schule* (Graz School).

Graz is interesting also because of the political climate surrounding its architecture. By the beginning of 1980s the local architects had managed to get strong political support from the governor of Styria, Josef Krainer.[14] His long moderate conservative rule lasted until the beginning of 1990s. It led to the reorganization of the social housing program and finally to a vast redevelopment program, including some dozen major university buildings, schools, and hospitals mostly in Graz and its environs. A majority of the projects were awarded through either limited or open competitions.[15] The Styrian competition program has been perhaps the most comprehensive in Europe and, at least until recently, the most progressive and experimental in its results. The opening in 1987 of the government-subsidized *Haus der Architektur* (House of Architecture), which organizes lectures, seminars, workshops, and exhibitions, sealed the political support for architecture and functions as a vivid forum for discourse.

Contemporary Austrian architecture is particularly interesting when compared with the other local tendencies that developed from the late 1970s on, for example in Ticino and Barcelona. Despite their different cultural and political frameworks, they all have been too frequently categorized simply as regional deviations of the mainstream. Kenneth Frampton's "Towards a Critical Regionalism," although focusing on an older generation of architects, offers an interesting point of reference for my discussion.

I hope that this book fills a gap in architectural criticism with respect to Austria's contribution to postwar architecture. Whereas most local (peripheral) developments in Austria still must be critically assessed (a few catalogs exist), several excellent studies cover Viennese postwar art and architecture. In the field of architecture, the Viennese visionary tendencies of the 1960s and 1970s are well documented in Günther Feuerstein's book *Visionäre Architektur Wien 1958–1988*, to name one. Viennese postwar architecture, which came into its own before that of Graz, is taken as a point of departure. The work of groups COOP Himmelblau and Haus-Rucker-Co among others will be discussed in relation to the Graz architecture scene.

Since my book focuses on works which I consider emblematic to the postwar cultural debate in Austria, I had to leave out an interesting body of work by what can be called the third generation of the Grazer Schule. Graz now has some 250 architectural offices, and the local scene that was once centered around a few restaurants (*Gasthäuser*) has become more fragmented. I have referred to the younger generation mostly through illustrations. The works of Fredl Bramberger, Arthur van der Broek, Martin Häusle, Wolfgang Feyferlik, and Francesco de Luca seem to indicate a direction toward which contemporary Austrian architecture might be heading.

This work owes much to Volker Giencke, the architect in whose office I first confronted the issues discussed here. I have written mainly about his work not only because I am most familiar with it or because, as I admit, I am personally attached to it, but because I am convinced that it is interesting in the same way that Graz itself is. Born after the war, Giencke belongs to the second generation of architects practicing in a period that follows the expansion of architectural culture into the realm of other arts that took place in the 1960s and 1970s. His work thus represents more subtle appropriations of postwar strategies than that of his predecessors. In addition, Giencke's architecture is nourished by the vivid dialogue with several of his contemporaries who shared ideas and architectural language. The works of Günther Domenig, Klaus Kada, and Helmut Richter give insight to the nuances of different approaches.

Giencke is a synthesizer rather than an innovator; his architecture is peripheral exactly due to this way of working within tradition and taking architecture beyond questions of any individual style. I believe that his oeuvre is of particular interest because he, unlike many others, avoided fixing his language: in architecture the form really doesn't matter after all.

Architecture as
an Event

Suggested act in street,
will police allow it, will police allow it,
I must say the atmosphere of modern streets is not theatrical,
therefore must,
find my environment, environment,
inclement weather, inclement weather
mobile theatre,
anyway you don't rehearse in the street,
anyway everything based on money,
and money or lack of it prevent everything,
one must be able to intimate materials do not cost anything:
timber, canvas, food and actors,
they can be got without money, or bartered, a commodity
co-operative can be re-established . . .

—**Antonin Artaud**

The Stage

The setup is simple: a spectacular urban square and a rectangular red sail rising to the rooftops of neighboring houses. The square is confined by undulating walls of two houses on both sides and by a steep cliff and the famous carved *Schloßbergstiege* (Schloßberg-stairs) in the back. The sail stands on the right-hand side of the square and is some 15 meters high and 7 meters wide. It is suspended both from the rock behind and sideways from the neighboring houses. Taking a closer look, one sees a low-stepped podium in front of the huge construction that marks a stage. It is a stage within a stage, in that the constructed spectacle conjoins with the natural spectacle of urban life. It was designed by Volker Giencke in the *Schloßbergplatz* in the heart of the inner city of Graz, the capital of the province of Styria in western Austria. The time was autumn of 1984.

The project was conceived for the annual art festival called Styrian autumn, known for its avant-garde reputation as a site for concerts relating to the festival. The project was born at the time when the international architecture scene was dominated by vernacular regionalism, postmodern classicism, neorationalism, eclecticism, and other trends and isms that opposed mainstream modernism.

Projects such as the Red Stage developed simultaneously with what came to be called postmodernism, and represented resistance to the cold formalism that had rendered much of modern architecture inhumane. Rather than turning away from the tradition of the modern, these new sensibilities developed critical strategies that used methods of negation against the modernist dogma by asserting an agenda that exceeds formal issues, yet remains within the orbit of modern aesthetics. What was at stake was the constitution of a new

Graz, view toward Schloßberg over the inner city

Volker Giencke, the Red Stage, Schloßbergplatz,
Graz, 1984

social and political agenda for architecture. What I call *engaged architecture* must be understood against the background of various counter-culture movements of the 1960s and 1970s, in which visual arts expanded into the realms of other disciplines such as film and theatre, learning from their politics and modes of representation. I believe that the most radical tendencies in contemporary European architecture today can still be understood in the context of liberation of arts that had its origin in the postwar intellectual climate characterized by new sexual politics and revolutionary rhetoric.

The names given to the work—*Die Rote Bühne; Tutuguri, ein Projekt für ein Total-Theater* ("The Red Stage; Tutuguri, A Project for Total Theatre")—recall both the German romantic tradition and the heritage of Nietzsche in Artaud's "Theatre of Cruelty." Total theatre is a useful metaphor. As a realm that combines different visual and acoustic elements in a way that opposes the hegemony of narrative and meaning, theatre becomes essentially antistructural. Conceived as such, theatre is released from the representational and enters

Architecture as

an Event

the realm of production and transformation; it aims to intensify life by reinventing itself rather than by depicting certain psychological states that lie outside. The names given to the Red Stage reflect the new tendencies: different visual practices are explored for critical reflection and for reassessing the social role of architecture. Rather than reducing architecture's role to problem solving, the work suggests architecture's capacity to become a protopolitical force in a society striving for the communal, for belonging.

Antonin Artaud's manifesto "Theatre of Cruelty" grew out of the surrealist tradition and was published in 1933. Artaud wrote, "Our long standing habit of seeking diversions has made us forget the slightest idea of serious theatre which upsets all our preconceptions, inspiring us with fiery, magnetic imagery and finally reacting on us after the manner of unforgettable soul therapy." [2] Following the surrealists, he aimed at a theatre that would possess the spectator totally; the spectator would lose control, indifference would turn into involvement. Artaud continues: "Everything that acts is cruelty. Theatre must rebuild itself on a concept of this drastic action pushed to the limit. . . . If theatre wants to find itself needed once more, it must present everything in love, crime, war and madness." [3]

This demand for total involvement through intensification recalls the surrealist's fascination with *image*. Surrealism is important for our discussion, as it is precisely its concept of the image that helps us to understand how it is tied to a particular social project based on engagement. Paul Mann discusses this revolutionary quality of the surrealist image as follows:

[Surrealism] wished to intensify the image, weakened by centuries of reasonable and correct analogy. . . . For Breton it is the violence with which reason is transgressed that drives the image into the unconscious and opens its utopia of desire for the revolution. [4]

Central to the surrealist understanding of an image is its ability to exceed the intellect and take us beyond the mere representational quality of an image. The surrealist image not only supports the sense of unreality, but intensifies the sense of an instant as the pure possession of an image. Intensification of the image is able to trigger desire leading from a mere contemplative and meditative relationship with the world into one of active engagement.

Against this background it is important to understand that Artaudian theatre is not based on the dichotomy between artifice and authenticity or between representation and the real, but rather on the concept of virtuality. Virtuality by its essence blurs the distinction between reality and the imaginary or unreal. Its aim is not to imitate reality but to create an alternative reality. Artaud described virtuality as "a purely assumed, dreamlike level" or "a mental field" that theatre is able to activate. What finally matters is the activated mental impact on the spectator rather than any narrative meaning, which traditional theatre attempts to transmit.

The Red Stage can be understood against Artaud's notion of virtuality as a hallucinatory vision—a *phantasm*. The image so created has the ability to manipulate, even transcend, reality by transforming the real into the imaginary and other way round. The social agenda is based on a fluid notion of the real that lacks permanent quality and can thus be altered easily; an image therefore is able to anticipate an alternative kind of reality.

The Red Stage can be understood against the two poles of postwar architectural debate: strategies proposed by high modernism on one hand and what I call engaged architecture on the other. During the 1950s architecture tried to tackle the ills of postwar crisis by creating a reified relationship between humans and the world through the celebration of sculptural form. By the 1960s, however, these reconstitutive practices of high modernism appeared rather ludicrous. There was growing awareness from the 1960s on that the problems of architecture could not be solved by understanding it as an autonomous object merely to be contemplated. Architecture had to go beyond mere aesthetic considerations and the visual to beat the postwar aporia. From then on the more critical strands sought new strategies for engagement and, perhaps, some kind of cure.

Informed by phenomenology, semiotics, and existentialism, as well as by Marxist critique, these new strategies started to engage with the critical and life-enhancing potentials of architecture that lie within the correspondence between architecture and the perceiver. The new sensitivity is based on the belief that architecture has the ability to transcend reality by transcending its own objecthood. So conceived it can never fully be possessed by a contemplating look, but rather evokes participation—even confusion—through its ambiguous relationship with the real. Both its critical and its generative potential lie in this ability to expand and create new realities.

The relocation of architecture and its social agenda involved going beyond the abstracted visual practices of high modernism, which had led architecture to become either a mere formal expression of the sculptural "psycho-poetics" (Connah) of space or, in the worst case, a merely pragmatic solution combining high efficiency with a weak compositional agenda. The strategies discussed here must be seen as separate from the so-called reconstitutive critical practices offered by Sigfried Giedion in *Space, Time and Architecture* and later by Kenneth Frampton in his essay "Towards a Critical Regionalism." [5] Frampton described tectonics as a strategy of resisting the homogenizing tendencies of modernism. This strategy is very similar to Giedion's space-time, proposed some thirty years earlier; Frampton's heightened sense of material experience is reminiscent of Giedion's space-time experience in that both aim at a reified relationship between humans and the world. The problem is that both men see the problem as lying within the object. By reconstituting the lost architecture—that of suppressed regional sensibilities in Frampton's case and spatiotemporal experience in Giedion's—a subject placed within an object would gain, as Michael Hays writes in his criticism of Giedion's thesis, an "experience of psychic gratification and integration to the world drained of it." [6]

As for Giedion, evocations of feeling and aesthetic "absorption" (Wörringer) become the moments of resurrection. In the examples of Jørn Utzon and Alvar Aalto, the architectural experience reaches its climax in the use of free form, in the individual gesture, like the undulating inner spatial contour of Utzon's Bagsvaed church and the structural extravaganza of the roof construction in Aalto's Säynätsalo assembly hall. Limited by the idea of an immediate sensuous-spatial experience, architecture falls into mere picturesqueness, into the unresolved dialectics of classical order and free form. It is understood as a framed still picture removed from the world. Architecture conceived as an isolated object supports a false consciousness of modern society.

The problem with the strategies offered both by Giedion and Frampton is that, to reconstitute the rift between humans and the world, the subject must be understood as "a centered subject" (Hays), an unaltered psyche facing the nonalienated reality. Michael Hays's discussion informs the ideological position of reconstitutive critical practices in his discussion of Giedion:

[But] in the intangible realm between inner and outer reality, between perceptual categories and modes of production, between subject and object, there remains something disturbing about Giedion's specific theory of modern architecture. For precisely at a time when reification was penetrating into the very core of personal experience, leaving no vestiges of a nonalienated reality as its reciprocal or opposing notion, Giedion's theory—which came into being as a protest and a defense against reification—emerged as the perpetuation of a conception of a historical moment, wholly present, in which the individual subject would somehow be fully conscious of his or her determination by such extrinsic structural conditions of modernity, and would somehow be able to reintegrate and resolve these determinations in the visual experience of architectural form. From Marx and Freud to recent poststructuralist theory, we have been shown again and again that such a resolution, such an immanence, is a myth, an ideological mirage. [7]

Alvar Aalto, Säynätsalo town hall, roof construction in the assembly hall,1952 (photo: H. Havas)

Frampton's thesis is of particular interest because it launched a discussion that took place parallel to the development of the new tendencies discussed here. His thesis has, in fact, been indirectly applied in several articles
to categorize those tendencies solely in terms of locality. Frampton promotes
the idea of regional tendencies, represented by local craftmanship and tectonics, as a means to resist the universal and homogenizing modernist rhetoric
represented by technology. I maintain that the body of work discussed here
reassesses the role of both tectonics and technology, and also challenges our
traditional understanding of the center-periphery hierarchy.

To clarify the difference between what Frampton calls critical regionalism and the new resistant tendencies in contemporary Austrian architecture,
I would like to introduce the following semantic shift: the move from locality
to the notion of the periphery. The concepts *periphery* and *peripheral* are important for our discussion: rather than implying the dichotomy between the
local and the universal, where the local traditions end up merely reaffirming
the position of the center (the universal and the mainstream), the peripheral
marks the breaking loose from such dichotomy.

The peripheral challenges traditional modes of architectural representation based on formal hierarchies and ordering principles. Yet it does not introduce a new formal language but goes beyond the traditional (modernist
and classical) understandings of form and space altogether. At the same time
the peripheral has several connotations: whether it is understood in terms
of geographical location, in relation to the modern tradition and modes of
representation, or even referring to minor names, the peripheral stands for a
certain freedom and a subtlety that offer an escape from easy categorization
or dichotomies.

Peripheral implies a synthetic approach: distinctions become blurred
when architecture exceeds mere formal and aesthetic considerations. The locus of this blurring is imagination and the imaginary; so conceived, the intensified image is emblematic of these peripheral notions. Rather than trying
to fix or settle architecture into any formal solution, the aim is to challenge
and questions the limits of architecture in general.

The peripheral tendencies, represented here by the Red Stage, use another kind of strategy opposed to that of spatial experience based on a dialectical relationship between subject and object. As an operational move,
opposed to the abstracted poetics of space and time, the space is sublated—
partly negated and later rediscovered. Architecture no longer offers the illusion of eternal presence represented by spatial enclosure, but instead, using
Heidegger's language, it "opens itself up to the world" as an image that has a

temporal dimension. Image is given priority over space so as to intensify the moment of confrontation.

The strategies of the image must be understood against the loss of social agenda of high modernism. By the 1960s the spatial emphasis in architecture had led into the blind alley of mere contemplation. The emphasis on the temporal represented by the image mandates active engagement against contemplation. To constitute a new social and political agenda, the relationship between the perceiver and architecture had to be reestablished. Phenomenology and existentialism offer a way out of the subject-object dichotomy. The idea of (mere) appearance, common especially in the Anglo-American philosophical tradition, was based on the supposition of an existing, unaltered reality distinct from the apparition of this reality as a mental construct produced by the onlooker. It was neglected in favor of a more dynamic relationship where this causal chain had to be broken.[8] This was achieved by going beyond the ideology of harmony and completeness represented by bounded space, and creating instead the image as a field of incompleteness and ambiguity. Architecture, therefore, rather than being a source of passive experience and contemplation, mandates engagement.

The Red Stage can be used to evaluate those tendencies in contemporary European architecture that have started to reassess and challenge the dogma of mainstream modernism and its modes of representation. The project also suggests a relocation of architecture's role in the society. These tendencies, of which the Red Stage is an introductory example, attempt to restructure the perception process by borrowing from other visual practices. At the same time these tendencies have started reassessment of the role of architectural meaning and signification.

In many ways the work does not fulfill most of the commonly held criteria of what architecture is, in fact, it contradicts established notions. The image quality of the work that is simultaneously simple and strange appears most dominant. This created image is more powerful than the presence of functional, structural, or spatial readings, which traditionally form the basis of architectural semantics. The "architectural" within the project, its structural and functional organization, remains concealed by the moment of confrontation. Despite this partial negation, these levels of signification are mysteriously present. The work first sublates and later rediscovers and relocates the architectural, that is, the role of structure and function. The image therefore marks this rediscovery.

By creating temporal suspense the Red Stage makes a strong statement about architecture in general and urban architecture in particular, emphasiz-

Haus-Rucker-Co, *Rahmenbau*, Documenta 6,
Kassel, 1977 (photo: Gert Winkler)

ing its essentially communal and urban qualities. The city and the architecture are again understood as sites of adventure, as places where things enter our lives without warning. In this case, a building is considered something that happens, involving the whole repertoire of sense perceptions connected with a happening.

Stepping outside the limits of traditional understanding proves to be a successful way of resisting the autonomous character of architectural objects, as well as a way of questioning the idea that architecture is constituted for a centered individual subject. By remaining within the architecture conceived as an object the so-called reconstitutive practices seemed to be adding to the fragmentation of modern society, in this case by creating an autonomous architectural experience separate from other experiences. The use of image enhances the experience of happening and collectivity, thereby helping to regain the impetus of architecture as a social art form. From this point of view, the work reveals techniques and strategies in contemporary architecture that help us, first, to locate the new tendencies within the architectural tradition per se; second, to reassess the role and possibilities of architectural signification and representation in relation to the larger field of visual practices; and third, to understand how these techniques and strategies are used to mandate engagement in order to regain architecture's role within society.

Rediscovering Architecture

The Red Stage manipulates perception. The work's signification lies outside the conventional architectural language; the encounter is filled with uncertainty concerning what has been encountered. The first encounter is dominated by astonishment, shock. The shock alone makes one think, and it is this ability to activate thinking that makes the rediscovery or reinvention of architecture possible.

Only the soon-to-be-discovered stage podium reveals the apparent function of the construction. Yet, it is the signification that lies outside the conventional that constitutes a feeling of something happening here. By erasing conventional architectural semantics, the meaning at the moment of encounter seeks to return to its natural indication of what an image, in this case a construction made of a red rectangular canvas rising as high as the rooftops in a public square, can tell us. This natural reading tells us about the most basic purposes of architecture: to enhance social and collective functions, and to create spaces for being together within buildings and in the city.

Engaged architecture looks for methods of going beyond the formal agenda, the spatiotemporal experience, to reevaluate the subject-object relationship and the possibilities of constituting a new social and political agenda for architecture. Going beyond autonomous visual practice demands the formerly discussed strategy of negation, which in the case of the Red Stage is marked by the substitution of the functional and spatial levels of meaning, which serve as emblems of the subject's control over the object, with an ambivalent image.

The work's ambiguity lies in the fact that the expected integrity of functional meaning is turned into an image substitute. It is based on the unresolved hierarchy between meaning, the eventual function of the construction as a bandstand, and the corresponding image. The image remains incomplete until the functional meaning has been (re)discovered. Until then the image-meaning dichotomy creates a new subject of architecture; no longer is it the moving and experiencing subject, but a subject that comes under the spell of suspense, desire, and waiting.

The Red Stage demonstrates a crucial strategy of avant-garde practice: sublation either through negation or through creation of ambiguity between different readings. The aims are to blur the hierarchy between image and referent, and to deny, at least partially, the hegemony of meaning, language, and structure. Instead of finding the referent behind the image, the image evokes imagination. The different strategies of sublation restructure the subject-object hierarchy, since only in so doing does architecture gain its social and political impetus.

The Red Stage introduces architectural image as a method of negation. The image can be understood as an avant-garde technique used to restructure the perception process. Negation, traditionally understood as "the dismantling of traditional formal conventions, the production of ruptures and discontinuities, the repudiation of the individual author as the originator of meaning, and the denial to the viewing subject of a space apart from life in which the mind is free to dream, to escape," writes Michael Hays, "is not just nay-saying; it is the active constructing of new perception, the forcing of a new situation through form." [9]

Deleuze's discussion of cinema relates to the function of image in architecture. He describes the shift from the so-called movement-image, dominated by action and spatial movement, to time-image, where time ceases to be subordinate to movement but "appears for itself." Time here does not appear as a representation of flowing presence as in the case of the movement-image, but becomes the subject itself in waiting, suspense, boredom, whatever. Time thus gains the dynamism that fluctuates between being and becoming: "time

Volker Giencke, the Red Stage

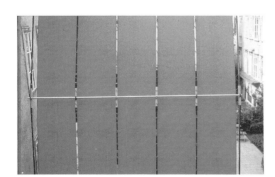

Architecture as

an Event

is full, that is, the unalterable form filled by change."[10] Deleuze gives the following explanation to the shift from movement-image to time-image: ". . . to prevent perception being extended into action in order to put it in contact with thought."[11] In architecture one can trace a similar development backed up by a similar intention: architecture understood as a social art form could not afford to offer mere spatiotemporal experiences.

Gaston Bachelard's discussion of the "psychic positivity of the image" describes this confrontational aspect of the image and its relationship to space; image is understood as a gate to imagination, whereas spatial experience is based on certain "disinterestedness" as described by the philosophies of the beautiful. Bachelard writes in *The Poetics of Space*: ". . . phenomenology can learn from the very brevity of the image. What strikes us here is that the metaphysical aspect originates on the very level of the image, on the level of an image which disturbs the notions of a spatiality commonly considered to be able to reduce these disturbances and restore the mind to a statute or indifference to space that does not have to localize dramatic events."[12] A similar dichotomy between space and image characterizes Deleuze's thesis: "We are not talking about dimensions of space, since the image may be flat, without depth, and though very flat it assumes all the more dimensions or powers which go beyond space."[13]

The rupture of the eternal flowing presence of space-time does not therefore mean simultaneous denial of all meaning, but rather relocation and reevaluation of that meaning. Therefore, despite its partial muteness, the image has the ability to evoke symbolic readings, which introduce a parallel system of signification that challenges those of conventional architectural language. The new mode of signification will be called *symbolic motivation* (Ricoeur), which instead of referring to any single meaning is able to create a mental field that tells us something about the character and disposition of the new architecture, that is, how architecture defines its relationship to society on both an individual as well as on a collective level: a certain ethos of architecture. This ethos is evoked by the natural signification within the image—an ambiance and gesture—which mandates an innocent reading.

A main premise for the return to image seems in accordance with what the surrealists were after. Already suggested by Freud's theory of the dream image and later developed by phenomenology, theories seeking out realms of such symbolic ambiguity have been central for thinkers who sought to challenge Cartesian rationalism. Similarly, in art and architecture, strategies of the image start to question any easy correspondence between form and content.

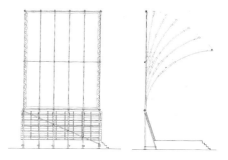

Volker Giencke, the Red Stage, section and back
elevation

The dominance of the image challenges the hegemony of language and the ideas of fixed structure and meaning. According to Roland Barthes, the image is the limit of language. Images are able to "imply, underlying their signifiers, a 'floating chain' of signifieds."[14] In other words, an image is inexhaustible and invites ever-different readings. The turn to image in literature—Thomas Mann's "Death in Venice" comes to mind—is the moment when the sensuous presence of some individual moment breaks the continuum of the narrative; the arrival of the image is the beginning of antistructure, degree zero. Image is a beginning of poetics; poetry begins where the single word gains thickness of meaning.

In Merleau-Ponty's terminology, the image provides the "circumscribed ignorance, that still 'empty' but already determinate intention which is attention itself."[15] Merleau-Ponty continues: "the first operation of attention is, then, to create for itself a field, either perceptual or mental, which can be 'surveyed' (*überschauen*), in which movements of the exploratory organ or elaborations of thought are possible, but in which consciousness does not correspondingly lose what it has gained and, moreover, lose itself in the changes it brings about."[16] Once made autonomous, the image has the ability to constitute a mood or field marked by the field of attention around itself. In the case of the Red Stage the mood is dominated by suspension and waiting for something to happen: ". . . something ought to happen 'around the image, behind the image, and even inside the image.'"[17]

Despite a certain muteness, image waits to be unveiled. One senses a stubborn presence of happening, both in the social and in the architectural sense. The unveiling in the case of the Red Stage becomes a rediscovery of function, structure, and space as architectural elements. Closer scrutiny reveals the subtle techniques of blurring symbolic and functional readings, and aesthetic and linguistic levels of the work. Yet the image maintains partial autonomy and silence among the different signification processes involved in the work.

The supporting construction for the sail was made of aluminium (primary construction) and of high-jump poles (secondary construction); the sail was mounted on the latter. The functional secret lies in the ability of the whole construction to bend, in case of rain, when the sail becomes a shelter, or for acoustic purposes, when it acts as a reflector. When bent, the structural, functional, and spatial qualities are revealed simultaneously. Transformation of the image into a functioning and tactile thing emphasizes the architectural. The transformed element, which now serves a practical purpose, maintains an unreal and imaginary quality, since works of architecture are not supposed to move. Architecture turns playful as the image becomes an event. Here it promotes what can be called a softened pragmatics, which can be understood as taking up a critical stance against the rational pragmatics of high modernism that instrumentalized architecture.

The work becomes a play between the symbolic and the functional levels in which we cannot clearly distinguish where one level begins and the other ends. Both levels are inherent in the image. The image has the ability to evoke emotions and action. Functionality grows from the dynamic interplay between the linguistic, the way the work conveys meaning, and the symbolic, the way the work motivates emotions and reactions.

The function of the Red Stage has an alternating character that cannot be reduced to the programmatic alone. The passage from image to the rediscovery of the architectural turns structure, function, and space into something re-presented. The Red Stage demonstrates that function and structure are not merely conceived as meaning inherent in the object, but as architecture's capacity to act. Similarly, rather than reducing it to sites for mere passive experience, architecture is meant to be enacted. This correspondence between acting and enacting, between subject and object, causes a reevaluation of architectural experience: rather than investing an architectural object with meaning, experience lies in architecture's ability to act in return. The produced meaning comprises programmatic and symbolic levels. One part of the function enhances the collectivity of an event that lacks a programmatic agenda, whereas the second level is activated by an excess of the symbolic level, which makes the crowds delight in their own dynamism, independent of any actual performance. In the end, functionality thus exceeds the limits defined by the linguistic signification per se.

What interests us here is this ability to expand the notion of signification. Architecture is transformed into a tactile image that carries the sensation of a happening. Even though the actual event has not yet occurred, its presence is tangible. Because it creates suspense and refuses disposition as a piece of equipment, architecture becomes an event—something taking place. By moving the emphasis from function to mood, the work is devoid of the instrumentality that makes it possible for the subject to control the object. The constitution of mood is due to the image's ability to create presence of architecture through its negation.

The event can then be characterized as the moment where potentiality transforms into possibility: the suspense is based on potentiality, which is marked by a certain lack inherent in the image. This suspense inhered in incompleteness constitutes desire, that is, anticipation and intensive participation in the moment to come. The constitution of desire makes architecture gain value through its operative function—how it works—rather than through "quasimetaphysical illusions of authenticity, unity, or depth." [18] Yet the newness combines both the fetish quality of the work and the innocence of the fantastic and the visionary. The essence of this desire is a longing for becoming. Desire understood as anticipation of the possible captures the essence of life: "There is in effect something that humans are and have to be," writes Giorgio Agamben, "but this something is not an essence nor properly a thing: It is simple fact of one's own existence as possibility of potentiality." [19]

This desire, when it involves an architectural event, breaks the distance expected between the work and a spectator; everyone in the end participates in the act. The longing was for the epiphany of a collective being together, a moment that manifests truly what urbanity means. The image-event becomes the ultimate architectural act enabling us to rediscover the moment when architecture comes into being.

The operational qualities of the image can be characterized by Heidegger's concept of "obtrusiveness" that talks about similar strategies of negation and sublation. They are all based on the ability to constitute lack and a moment of its realization; in the case of the Red Stage, it is the rediscovery of the collective and functional (architectural) meaning of the work. Obtrusiveness demands that the matter of the work also "resist," in Heidegger's words, "perishing in the equipmental being of the equipment." [20] Manipulating the absence, constructing a lack, is essential. That is how the Red Stage operates: by suspending the discovery of the architectural—function and structure—within the image, it enables us to live through and participate in the birth of architecture.

The image can therefore be judged as constituted by both emptiness and potentiality. We can borrow Giorgio Agamben's words to describe the passage from image to rediscovery, from the potentiality, from "not-be," into potentiality, into "to-be," as follows:

Everything rests here on the mode in which the passage from potentiality to act comes about. The symmetry between the potentiality to be and the potentiality to not-be is, in effect, only apparent. In the potentiality to be, potentiality has as its object a certain act, in the sense that for it energhein, being-in-act, can only mean passing to a determinate activity (this is why Schelling defines the potentiality that cannot not pass into action as blind); as for the potentiality to not-be, on the other hand, the act can never consist of a simple transition de potentia ad actum: It is, in other words, a potentiality that has as its object potentiality itself, a potentia potentiae. [21]

Agamben recalls Heidegger's idea of obtrusiveness: "Only a power that is capable of both power and impotence, then is the supreme power."[22] The task set for the new architecture is to make the impotence of mere possibility visible and transform it to potentiality. The Red Stage is also a statement for particularity in the sense that the self-evidence of belonging to a category, in this case the category of architecture, is being neglected. Instead, it forces us to restate the question of what architecture is in the first place. The general exists only through the notion of singularity based on the capacity to be otherwise.

The Zone: Techniques of Dislocation

The image is in itself a nodal point where ambiguities are produced. It is a starting point for discovery, *a zone* for working against and within. Therefore, an architectural image is not a point of arrival, but a point of departure.

The image creates a dynamic subject-object correspondence by fighting the hegemony of language as the preexisting referent. It provides a certain emptiness by transfiguring time. The encounter, or "the empty moment" to borrow Duchamp's words, ". . . is a sort of rendezvous."[23] In a way the image has the ability to create a moment of condensed time and break the abstract notion of time as a flowing continuum, which is the underlying conceptual premise of modernist architectural space. Whereas time as a continuum can be measured, for example, as movement, condensed time presents itself as a mental state. The rendezvous can be the result of an image understood as Deleuzian "Noosign": "The image which goes beyond itself towards something which can only be thought."[24] Deleuze also helps to illuminate this Heideggerian project of the image: ". . . it is the suspension of the world, rather than the movement which gives the visible to the thought."[25]

To enter the realm of thought means to enter into a ground common to both the producer and the perceiver where architecture comes into being. The techniques of the image are based on this ability to recall endlessly the moment of production. In Merleau-Pontian terms, architecture could be understood as speech rather than language, the latter carrying too strong a syntactical emphasis. Merleau-Ponty writes: "Speech and thought would admit of this external relation only if they were both thematically given, whereas in fact they are intervolved, the sense being held within the word, and the word being the external existence of the sense."[26] In this case architecture does not carry preexisting meaning by becoming the expression of thought, but rather it accomplishes thought.

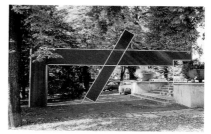

Thought returns us to the notion of virtuality, creating a possible world distinct from the one we call real. In this context, the revival of the Artaud's concept of total theatre can be understood as the creation of the poetic "if" [27]: the task of poetics is to make manifest that which does not yet exist by revealing potentialities. Compared with the idea of artifice and false consciousness of art, virtuality was the harbinger of better politics. The poetics conceived as potentiality becomes a political act.

Through this notion of poetics the image, unlike the self-sufficient architecture based on spatiotemporal experience, reflects the "thought horizon" (Merleau-Ponty) and cannot therefore be traced to any single source or meaning; it remains hybrid, interwoven with the productive process. Whereas the architecture of formal intentions is trapped in the isolation of an object as the carrier of posited meaning, engaged architecture mandates the creation of meaning. Against this field, architecture gains its dynamism and its ability to restructure the subject-object relationship.

The Red Stage uses reduced geometries to create an image. The reason might be that the geometries prompt us to stretch the possibilities of form, allowing for shifts of framework and reference. Form has to have this expansive quality; that is, it has to fight becoming static and enclosed before it can gain the character of an image. The strategy of reduced geometries is vague enough to allow any meaning or reference to be attached to form, and it therefore allows continuous shifting and displacement.

Another important strategy for dislocation is the intensification of materiality, texture, and color. Architecture reduced to tactile image can be understood as an intensification of energy and therefore of potentiality, rather than as something already located and defined by abstract geometrical systems of notation. An intensified sense of materiality is an essential quality of the image, heightening its presence by compressing time into an instant.

This sense of materiality is thus a constant ground for change; its essence lies always outside the form. Raw materiality emphasizes the production process rather than the complete object. The perceiver thus enters the construction of meaning. The consistent resistance of objecthood constitutes the basis of heterogeneity and depends on the ability to maintain a level of intensive materiality. Materiality rejects all functional, linguistic, and mimetic justifications. Obtrusiveness of the image makes the material "come forth" (Heidegger) in a sense that supports material qualities as they appear; for example, red is allowed to be nothing but red. The image is a decisive operational item that makes architecture into an event of making; of poesis. Materiality echoes the thought and together they form what film maker Jean-Luc

Volker Giencke, *Indianer—Art between the Wars in Graz,* exhibition installation, entrance

Opposite: Frederick Kiesler, two-part nesting table, 1935–1938 (collection Mrs. Isobel Grossman)

Aino and Alvar Aalto, Savoy vase, 1937

Godard called the "poetic structure" of architecture. Godard writes, "the poetic structure of the film, a thought that is, of managing to define that thought as an object, of seeing whether or not that object is living, and of eliminating the dead . . ."[28]

The reduced geometries, used mostly in combination with an intensified sense of material, texture, and color, define a new noncategory of architecture that Giorgio Agamben characterized as architecture based on singularity. No qualities are used for some particular end, but rather as means in themselves, in the straightforward manner of "such as it is," where direct contact with the environment gains importance. Properties such as color, material, and textuality gain an independent quality, rather than being mainly attributes for architecture.[29] Properties conceived as self-referential become fetishistic; their very being has a direct relation to desire. It is therefore the restrained elegance of reduced geometries and the heightened sense of materiality that constitute architecture that matters.

A striving for heterogeneity is the common denominator of contemporary tendencies in art and architecture. Postmodern classicism and deconstruction shared the use of fragment, collision, and collage to rid architecture of homogeneity and undesired unity and harmony. These strategies fight integrity through techniques of collage based on understanding architecture as something embodied in form. The limitation of collage is that it too often sacrifices heterogeneity for static arbitrariness. The strategy of dislocation, on the contrary, is based on a certain fluidity embodied in the image that is essential to maintaining the constantly shifting visual emphasis and discursive framework.

The second difference is that whereas collage takes place in an almost scientific conception of time and space, displacement happens in real time and place. In collage the concept of time is fragmented and discontinuous. Therefore collage has to be rejected for the same reason Godard rejected it: "Things depend on a passage of time."[30] This inability to capture the flow of time was a basis for futurists' criticism of cubism. The Red Stage achieves heterogeneity by a strategy of continuous displacements in real time. Architecture based on displacement differs from that of collage in that it is not something rigidly defined by form to be deciphered later. The attitude toward time makes architecture, to a certain degree, automatically resist form as something rigid. Architecture has more to do with a certain radiance beyond the form. In other words, it begins when its objecthood, the formal enclosure, is challenged by the aura of happening and the hybridity caused by displacement.

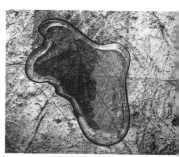

The type of architecture represented by the Red Stage is based on an ambiguity of image that fixes its statement without turning it into a static formalism. Therefore, one must make a clear distinction between form as limit and form as *boundary*. The strategy of reduced geometries can be located in the latter category: simple form is understood as boundary not limit. Architecture transformed into an image produces a "liminal" zone (Viktor Turner), which task is to produce ambiguities. Architecture becomes a site for resistance to the hegemony of a single dominant organizing principle, that is, the idea bounded space, by questioning the limits of architectural meaning. As Bernice Martin points out in his book on the strategies of the counter-culture of the 1970s, boundaries are ". . . important not merely because they hold the real in place but also because they are the locus of blessed as well as dangerous ambiguity."[31] George Simmel's understanding of the boundary takes us even farther to the realm of the dangerous. Simmel writes in "Metaphysics of Death": "the secret of form is that it is a boundary; it is the thing itself and, at the same time, the cessation of the thing, the circumscribed territory in which the being and the non-being of the thing are only one thing."[32] Simmel informs the concept of image as follows: the image conceived as a nondefinite form touches on and questions its own being, and thus the very being of architecture. The physical being of architecture ceases to concern itself with eternity, but mirrors the fragility of life itself.

Heidegger makes a similar distinction when describing the difference between something "fixed in place" and that which becomes "rigid" and "motionless." He writes:

"Fixed" means outlined, admitted into the boundary (peras), brought into the outline. The boundary in the Greek sense does not block off; rather, being itself brought forth, it first brings to its radiance what is present. Boundary sets free into the unconcealed; by its contour in the Greek light, the mountain stands in its towering and repose. The boundary that fixes and consolidates is in this repose—the repose in the fullness of motion—all this holds of the work in the Greek sense of ergon; this work's "being" is energeia, which gathers infinitely more movement within itself than do the modern "energies."[33]

Boundary depicts the ambiguity of presence, a culmination point for architecture no longer informed by meaning (knowledge) but by feeling and thought. The secrecy within the image urges action rather than passive contemplation.

The strategy of displacement is demonstrated by the dynamism between image and background—the urban site. The Red Stage creates uncertainty

Below: Ludwig Mies van der Rohe, project for a
glass skyscraper, ground floor plan

Ludwig Mies van der Rohe, project for a glass
skyscraper, Berlin, 1922, elevation

about the hierarchy and relationship between the work and its location. The
reorganization of space constituted by the image-sail is no longer based on
closure and movement, but on opening up an instant. This creates ambiguity,
regardless of whether or not the Red Stage creates synthesis or discontinuity
in its surroundings: the instant (image) gains importance over the movement
suggested by the urban setting. Yet this instant is simultaneously capable of
restructuring the spatial and functional qualities of the place to constitute a
sense of happening. The successful juxtaposition of the urban site and the red
sail construction forms a unity where neither has priority. In one sense the
red sail contradicts the historical site and stands therefore as dominant; in
another, it is subsumed by its own internal contradiction, the tension between the natural and manmade environment. The added element, the sail,
transforms the preexisting situation by exaggeration and contrast.

Architecture strives in this case for "negative contextualism."[34] As Massimo Cacciari pointed out, this negative dialectic tries to establish as central
what is actually eccentric. Similarly, the hidden qualities of the urban setting
are brought to the fore. Following the same logic, architectural form cannot be determined by an architectural focus or center, but always refers and
surprises by that which actually seems accidental, random, and irrelevant, by
shifting the focus. The work becomes an "essential supplement" (Agamben).
The supplement denies the enclosure and finitude of a given situation and
without actual alterations has the ability to make an essential difference—

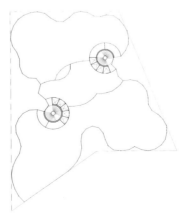

Gothic double-spiral staircase at the Burg, Graz

Volker Giencke, student house at Lendplatz, Graz,
1984, stair

"tiny dislocation." [35] The supplement is thus the ultimate strategy for negativity, denying the totality and closure of any system and the hegemony and center of any organizing principle.

Innocence Lost (The Cow Project)

The Cow Project took place in 1985 in Vogelsberg, Germany. Designed by the group Formalhaut—consisting of two architects, Götz Stöckmann and Gabriela Seifert, and a sculptor, Ottmar Hörl, from Frankfurt—it provides yet another example of how the technique of dislocation is able to capture ambiguous temporal conditions. The installation shares with Giencke's Red Stage a common ground that provides a basis for comparison.

What connects the two works is the particularity of the image that transmits a public and general idea that touches an individual through the problematics of the collective. They do this through raising key questions about urbanity and the urban environment, as in the case of the Red Stage, and by insinuating an environmentalist reading, as in the case of the Cow Project. Particularity is achieved through the curious combination of a certain strangeness and simplicity. Both works use the image as a means to resist the conventional and the compositional, the falling from incompleteness to completion; in other words, to stay close to life.

The image captures a picturesque landscape with some cows in a random herd trapped in transparent, rectangular, cow-sized containers. The landscape is more an emblem of paradise than a reminder of exploitation of land. Both the landscape and the cows convey the image of an unspoiled site. The transparent sheds freeze this pastoral image into an unchanging and timeless state. The sheds, transform the benign harmony of the landscape into an uncanny state of what seems like a slow-motion suffocation not unlike the ambiance in Gerhard Richter's paintings; that is, the familiar turning into the uncanny. Unlike the Red Stage, which captures a moment of becoming, the Cow Project remains in a state of pure being, demonstrating therefore the impossibility of becoming.

The knowledge that the project was done right before the nuclear catastrophe in Chernobyl gives the work another dimension: the highest levels of radiation were found in cows' milk. The political statement is subtle: the sheds at once provide shelter and demonstrate our changing relation to the landscape. And the cows! Once considered objects with exchange value, they now are frozen into objects of rare value that need protection.

Desire, which in the case of the Red Stage was the manifest desire for becoming, is here turned into nostalgia and remembrance of lost innocence.

Formalhaut, the Cow Project, Vogelsberg,
Germany, 1985 (photo: Alexander Beck)

Opposite: Gerhard Richter, *Cow,* 1964

Gerhard Richter, *Wiesental,* 1985

The dislocation is achieved by juxtaposition of the transparent, almost non-existent cow shelters with a perfectly normal bucolic picture, creating a shift in attitude and urging other readings. It is accomplished by inverting the perfectly normal and the uncanny. Yet the cows also trigger spontaneous laughter, which releases the project from any aesthetic aura; the spectator is allowed to enjoy the simple pleasures of the absurd and banal. The fluctuation between seriousness and humor culminates in laughter, demonstrating their coexistence in the absurd.

The cows are a deliberate choice. Should they be displaced by other animals or human beings, the installation would lose its critical edge. The cows convey the idea of timeless time, of a gently flowing present without the dimensions of past, present, or future: "All history looks pretty much the same to cows" (John Irving); nature is used to escape the dominance of history, of the separation of past, present, and future. The poor beast is known for its slowness; it exists only in the present. The Cow Project captures in a critical manner the task confronting new European architecture. Architecture can no longer represent the innocence of the eternally flowing present as movement within the equally innocent, white(!) spaces of the early masters. This innocence has become trapped in a timeless time having no relationship to the outer world. Despite the common technique of the supplement, that is, something superimposed and added to the preexisting, the two projects reveal a deep discrepancy. Whereas the Red Stage used its supplement status as an element mandating engagement, the Cow Project sublates the most essential element for this operative move: the dialectic of being and becoming is frozen into the eternal presence of timeless time.

Both examples show how displacement introduces a new dimension of time into architecture. It is not that of abstract spatiotemporal experience in timeless time conceived by the space-time experience, but that of the dialogue between being and becoming in a present moment, which lies within the work itself as it reifies real time.

The contrast demonstrated by the two projects suggests, for better or for worse, two possibilities for architecture. The contrast between the color of the Red Stage versus the transparency, the almost nothing, of the sheds turns out to be crucial. The Red Stage seems to force attention to the abundant possibilities—colors—of the world to be explored by reactivating people and the site. The transparency does the opposite, suffocating what was once a symbol of life and nourishment; the familiar turns uncanny.

The Cow Project is a negation of the Red Stage; it has an edge of pessimism to it, conveying the possibility that it could also be otherwise. The Red

Stage is full of faith in the capacity of architecture to make a difference. As innocence is lost, architecture has perhaps no other task than to become, embodying hope and reifying time as expectation, the last fortress of faith for a better world. Its problem therefore is how to participate in the constitution of a better politics rather than perpetrate false consciousness. Facing the same question, Gilles Deleuze writes: ". . . which, then, is the subtle way out? To believe, not in a different world, but in a link between man and the world, in love or life, to believe in this as in the impossible, the unthinkable, which none the less cannot but be thought: 'something possible, otherwise I will suffocate.' It is this belief that makes the unthought the specific power of thought, through the absurd, by virtue of the absurd." [36] Instead of depicting innocence lost, architecture should participate in reinventing innocence as a means to celebrate that virtue.

The New Utopia

The architecture of becoming can be understood as an event, as potentiality turning into possibility. The notion of an architectural event opposes the fragmentation and chaos of modern existence by constituting an "instant that takes hold of the chaos." [37] The simplest argument is Godard's: ". . . one can say, after an event, 'I have lived.'" [38]

Image, as the embodiment of the potentiality within an instant, contains the idea of the "not-yet" that Ernst Bloch, in *Das Prinzip Hoffnung*, described as utopian consciousness, already embedded in the real. Event can be understood as something that produces an alternative reality, something oriented toward the future. The senses of intensified time and being alive are heightened by image that exists as an event interweaving and superimposing them onto the real, and producing visionary effects that allow architecture even in a built form to retain a certain virtual quality.

Architecture conceived as an image, as an event, is utopian in its ability to awaken imagination and anticipate future acts. It exceeds the static character of determined form; it becomes ec-static and undetermined, bespeaking desire more than intent.

This utopian dimension demands an epistemological slant. We can no longer approach architecture as a representation of being or reality, the essence of which lies in simple presence or self-evidence of modernist space. Rather, we must approach it as an event coming into being, which materially echoes the real that always has a temporal dimension.

Strategies of displacement and supplement based on negation can therefore be developed even further. The crucial difference between these subtle strategies of negativity and the more absolutist rhetoric of earlier avant-gardes is that the former must be understood as productive rather than representational. Julia Kristeva's concept of negativity informs the techniques discussed above: "Negativity is not reified directly as lack or as the impossible real: it is reintroduced into every reality (réel) already posited to expose it to other realities, make it dynamic, and effect its *Aufhebung* in an endless mobility— positing elements (time or rest), reactivating the whirlwind (time of the crossing)."[39] The strategy of displacement should therefore be thought of as something that provides the overture for new possibilities to emerge within the real. What is proposed here is a new strategy for utopia, a shift of attitude, rather than a radical change of the physical environment as such. In utopia, the world to come is where "everything will be as it is now, just a little different" (Benjamin).

The utopian strategy of the Red Stage is grounded in the ability to recall the already existing, yet forgotten or suppressed, understanding of the city dweller as political animal. This notion becomes reactivated as a protopolitical force that resists the alienating forces of life in the metropolis as discussed by Georg Simmel. The resistance of these forces cannot rely merely on eliminating difference, but creates a sort of singularity based on hybridity where differences collapse when "so be it" and "otherwise" intermingle. In his book, *The Coming Community*, Giorgio Agamben writes:

The tiny displacement does not refer to the state of things, but to their sense and their limits. It does not take place in things, but at their periphery, in the space of ease between everything and itself. This means that even though perfection does not imply a real mutation it does not simply involve an external state of things, an incurable "so be it." On the contrary, the parable introduces a possibility there where everything is perfect, an "otherwise" where everything is finished forever, and precisely this is its irreducible aporia. But how is it possible that things be "otherwise" while everything is definitively finished?[40]

Benjamin's "just a little different" will be informed by the limits and new possibilities produced by the utopian instinct. Agamben continues:

One can think of the halo, in this sense, as a zone in which possibility and reality, potentiality and actuality, become indistinguishable. The being that has reached its end, that has consumed all of its possibilities, thus receives as a gift a supplement possibility.[41]

Agamben, borrowing from Ernst Bloch, provides a new utopia, or rather a utopian instinct, that lies within the existing society that provides a certain hybridity. His theory of dislocation can be compared with the concept of "heterotypia" proposed by Michel Foucault. Foucault's idea can be drawn back to the visual notion of collage: the "counter sites" proposed are "sites which have the curious property of being in relation with all other sites, but in such a way as to suspect, neutralize, or invent the set of relations that they happen to designate, mirror or reflect."[42] His heterotypia is based on spatial dislocation, which easily ends up being trapped in constant set of dichotomies.[43] Agamben, on the other hand, leads us to the more subtle strategy of constituting utopia: the essential supplement reveals the limits and the sense of things, peripheral, the otherwise. This surpasses the need for the complete negation of the state of things.

The Red Stage demonstrates the strategy of this new utopia. The universalizing forces of twentieth-century architecture are neglected in favor of constituting singularities. Opposed to the concept of the particular, which assumes a center, singularity, writes Agamben, "is thus freed from the false dilemma that obliges knowledge to choose between the ineffability of the individual and the intelligibility of the universal."[44] The strategy of constituting singularities is based on the potentiality of things to be otherwise by adding a temporal horizon to the state of things.

. . . Wir wollen Architektur, die mehr hat. Architektur, die blutet, die erschöpft, die dreht und meinetwegen bricht. Architektur, die leuchtet, die sticht, die fetzt und unter Dehnung reißt. Architektur muß schluchtig, feurig, glatt, hart, eckig, brutal, rund, zärtlich, farbig, obszön, geil, träumend, vernühend, verfernend, naß, trocken und herzschlagend sein. Lebend oder tot. Wenn sie kalt ist, dann kalt wie ein Eisblock. Wenn sie heiß ist, dann so heiß wie ein Flammenflügel.

Architektur muß brennen.[1]

—**COOP Himmelblau**

How to Construct Desire?

It is no surprise that the famous *Flammenaktion* ("flame action") by the Viennese COOP Himmelblau had to take place in Graz, as Wolfgang Prix and Helmut Swiczinsky of COOP Himmelblau found sympathy and friends among the architects there. By that time the architects in Graz had started to challenge what they themselves called the dull and rigid academism that dominated the architectural scene of Vienna. By the early 1980s the Viennese had gone hopelessly postmodern despite the promise in the 1970s of something more vivid. This left a group such as COOP Himmelblau almost alone in their search for an architecture that burns (and yearns?). By burning a piece of construction mounted on top of a crane in front of the Technical University of Graz as part of Professor Günther Domenig's inauguration ceremony in 1980, they manifested, among other things, their own distance from the capital's postmodern classicism.

What were the architects who joined to celebrate the *Flammenaktion* with COOP Himmelblau really opposing by wanting architecture to have more and to burn? Were Prix and Swiczinsky suggesting a rebirth, a zero degree of architecture in relation to history, or did they want peripheral architecture, a different relation toward architectural signification altogether? The motto "architecture must burn" and the act itself suggest several things. The act of burning architecture can imply both erasure and something more life-enhancing, such as ritual, feast, or warmth. Being a sign of both destruction and gentleness, as Heidegger points out, a flame captures the relations among life, memory, and history as the ambiguity inherent in the human condition. To quote Heidegger in his discussion of Trakl:

In his last poem, "Grodek," Trakl speaks of the "hot flame of spirit." The spirit is flaming, and only in this sense perhaps is it something flickering in the air. Trakl sees spirit not primarily as pneuma, something ethereal, but as a flame that inflames, startles, horrifies, and shatters us. Flame is glowing lumination. What flame is the ekstasis which lightens and calls forth radiance, but which may also go on consuming and reduce all to white ashes.[2]

COOP Himmelblau, The Blazing Wing, Graz,
1980

The *Flammenaktion* can be understood in this context: the flame is an emblem of spirited architecture that can move us, take us out of the everyday, and make us transcend ourselves. Heidegger continues:

Spirit is flame. It glows and shines. Its shining takes place in the beholding look. To such a vision is given the advent of all that shines, where all that is, is present. This flaming vision is pain. The nature remains impenetrable to any mind that understands pain in terms of sensitivity. Flaming vision determines the soul's greatness. The spirit which bears the gift of the "great soul" is pain; pain is the animator. and the soul so gifted is the giver of life. This is why everything that is alive in the sense in which the soul is alive, is imbued with pain, the fundamental trait of the soul's nature. Everything that is alive is painful. [3]

Architektur muß brennen can be understood as a plea that architecture must possess a spirit in order to depict the ambiguity of the human condition. The flame reassesses the social role of architecture. It is not something that aims solely at reconciliation and harmony, either between humans and the world by promoting merely reflective, supportive, and noncontradictory relationships between architecture and its surroundings or, more generally, between architecture and its social and cultural context. Rather, the new architecture suggested by COOP Himmelblau wants to intervene and disrupt so as to regain the power to which it is entitled.

The act of burning informs us about the attributes given to architecture in the manifesto: contradiction, transformation, movement, and change. Architecture must take place rather than merely be; the manifesto demands that it respond and that it be both desirable and desiring. Therefore, rather than suggesting a simple zero degree or tabula rasa, the manifesto must be read as a plea for architecture to provide discontinuity and difference, not by eliminating the already existing and the difference within it, but by adding difference, excess, the surplus of more. As much as the manifesto pleads for a new kind of architecture, it seems to add variety and meaning. COOP Himmelblau joins Adorno in the belief that art, to be effective, needs this duality of simultaneous negation and affirmation of accepted values. Through this attitude, new architecture participates in the critical undercurrents within twentieth-century architectural tradition that were born out of the reevaluation of the avant-garde project, thus demonstrating belief in the validity of such a project. Architecture has to fight the cultural status quo, and it has to be questioned continuously to stay alive.

This demand for excess as *geil, obzön*, and *heiß* (lustful, obscene, and hot) also refers obviously also to the realm of *Sinnlichkeit* (sensuality), of Eros, which allows room for play and fantasy, and therefore makes architecture exceed the reality principle. Following the tradition of modern aesthetics that started with Schiller, the sensuous play acts as a realm of reconciliation between humans and the world. Through play the excess becomes the realm of politics; the surplus gives the work both a Freudian and a utopian Marxist twist of fantasy as a realm where the psychological not-yet is activated. The excess denies the self-referentiality of a mere aesthetic object, but by provoking the not-yet, it points outside and evokes transformation and change. Architecture as event is motivated by the Heideggerian concept that uncovering possibilities makes the "what-lies-ahead-of-itself,"[4] or that which is still to be settled, dominate the present. The emphasis on both temporality and fantasy emphasizes the presence of an anticipating and *desiring subject*.

The manifesto must be understood in opposition to the closure of objects of pure being, that is, objects of mere aesthetic value and pure visibility, enclosed in their silent presence, which only add to the fragmentation of society. Architecture has to be more to regain its psychic dimension and reciprocal ability. COOP Himmelblau's demand that it respond can be understood against this background: architecture that is able to occupy the liminal zone, that of transformation and play, must embody a temporal presence that transforms the object into the other, who is able to look back at us, as suggested by Sartre.[5] This relationship between subjects and the world simultaneously transforms space into an oriented, existential space of desire. Following Merleau-Ponty's definition of the difference between an object and a thing,[6] architecture, rather than being an object, becomes a thing that is able not only to attract, which would turn it into a mere item of consumption, but also to repel.

Therefore light, which celebrates the beautiful by making an aesthetic object visible, is turned into flame and warmth, transforming the disinterested aesthetic object into an interested object. This enables the restoration of desire, lost intimacy, and lost love, as discussed by Karsten Harries.[7] A flame also has a temporal dimension that light lacks; it is able to repel. The demand for sensuality in "architecture must burn" differs from the merely visual in its warmth and its responsiveness. Harries proposes that the beautiful, understood as the object of an entirely disinterested satisfaction by Kantian aesthetics, at this point separates itself from the world, from the "desire to reality," and from "our usual involvement of time," and therefore anticipation. The excess that the manifesto describes as a realm of potentiality and change, appears as a demand to reconstitute the lost object of desire that, by manifesting the unfolding of time, can emancipate the feelings of the desiring subject, of the person in the world.

What then constitutes architecture that has more? One must remain sensitive to nuance: what is demanded is not based on "less is a bore," that is, not on demanding more of architecture, but on architecture that has more.[8] Making the same point with Nietzschean emphasis, the perceiver is called to enjoy the architecture of excess rather than the excess of architecture. The former implies intimacy, the erotic, and sensuality, architecture beyond the reality principle. The latter adds to the leveling of experience, ending with Hollein's idea that "everything is architecture," and recalling the euphoria of media and simulation during the communication mania of the late 1960s and 1970s, which culminated in the distanced irony of postmodern classicism and its emblem, the decorated shed.

The intentions of COOP Himmelblau and others who agreed with their manifesto join the tradition of twentieth-century avant-gardes following the surrealist heritage, which is based on the idea that the real revolutionary potential lies exactly within the subjective realm. The dominant energies of desire, the longing for love and life, can never become totally sublimated and taken over by modern society. These perhaps peripheral concepts of twentieth-century architecture first find mature expression in the dreaming, desiring subject of surrealism attempting to create a dynamic and transformative relationship with the world through imagination and fantasy. The act relies not solely on what is, but on what can be imagined—the more. Therefore the conclusion might be that ". . . the alienation of the spectacle is not complete: the passion to create reveals the persistence of desires for self-realization; love reveals the will for real communication; the play reveals the desire for free and chosen forms of participation in the world. And there are moments, be they poetic or erotic, which seem to represent some pure pole of authenticity which will always survive the vacuous equivalence of commodity relations."[9]

In the arts, this leads to the relocation of the subject: the knowing subject turns into a desiring subject. The reevaluation of perception by existentialism and phenomenology eliminates the distinction between consciousness and physical being, between mind and body. Merleau-Ponty's *Phenomenology of Perception*, which responds to Sartre's *Being and Nothingness*, participates in the constitution of the new subject, which becomes the basis of the new critical practices: "Let us try to see how a thing or a being begins to exist for us through desire or love and we shall thereby come to understand better how things and being can exist in general."[10] The new subject, rather than being a disembodied thinker, is understood as a "power, which is born into, and simultaneously with a certain existential environment, or is synchronized with it." [11] We return to the contrast between these critical tendencies and the reconstitutive tendencies of mainstream modernism. The latter constitute strategies based on the humanist eternal subject, whereas the former deny the collectivization of human experience and are based on the demands of desiring subject.

Working within the avant-garde tradition, these critical practices must show how architecture can help to constitute a free-acting subject. The dilemma has two faces; as Sartre understood, "there is freedom only in a situation, and there is a situation only through freedom." [12] The only way out is to turn architecture into an event, a ritual space, where similar interdependence exists: there is no event and no ritual without the experiencing subject. The work is therefore both the object of desire and the constitutive element of that desire. This double function requires a temporal element, the ability to activate a process, and a certain open-endedness that not only enables repetition of the act of transformation, but allows the work to unfold endlessly. This means that the architecture that has more, as well as the object of desire, should never become something taken for granted. *Spirited* architecture can be understood as *poetic* architecture, as capturing ambiguity and having a psychic dimension. Architecture becomes ecstatic; it trembles.

Architecture *mise en* Landscape

In Graz the demand for excess found different expressions than in Vienna. Maybe Günther Domenig's architectural language, Z-Bank is emblematic, is closest to the explosive and expressive structures of COOP Himmelblau: buildings breaking off from the greyness of their surroundings. With this virtually total negation of contextuality and continuity, this total disrupture, Graz started to produce more subtle strategies of creating difference through the dialectic relationship between architecture (the supplement) and the existing surroundings. Known for his transformative gestures as demonstrated by the Red Stage, Giencke became one of the main proponents of these actions. The study of the dialectic between landscape and architecture became a primary agenda that allowed him constantly to blur the hierarchy between figure and ground, to set the relationship between architecture and landscape in tension.

At the time of *Flammenaktion*, Giencke was still a newcomer. Only in his midthirties, he had already built the drydock on *Wörthersee* in Klagenfurt. The building is dominated by the horizontal steel truss that supports the movable crane horizontally and becomes a datum against the background of the majestic Karawanken Mountains. Constructed like an artificial island, this first

Günther Domenig, Z-Bank, Vienna, 1979

built project shows Giencke's unorthodox way of combining different architectural languages and his mastery of intelligent technical solutions. The work shows his interest in a dynamic relationship between landscape and architecture. The underwater service facilities form an artificial island on which the building "takes place"; architecture starts by making the land(scape) its podium. Giencke's interest in the duality of *Gebaute Landschaft—Landschaft als Bauform* ("built landscape—landscape as built form")[13] reveals his ideology; he departs from the hierarchy of nature first and architecture second, but he understands the dialectics of the process. As the quotation shows, he constantly blurs the boundary between landscape and architecture.

Giencke's next major project, the glasshouses for the botanical garden in Graz, dates from 1982, two years after the *Flammenaktion*. The glasshouses further elaborate the dialectics between architecture and landscape. At the same time, as a built work it retains a curiously visionary character, something that can be said about few other projects, no matter how outrageous they may be when they reach the built stage.

Let us take a closer look at this work, which was acclaimed internationally while still a project, and for which Giencke is most known. Confusion is manifest within the architectural community when it confronts projects such as the glasshouses, which shun easy categorization. An indicator of this, pro or con, seems to be figurative interpretations. In his book, *New Spirit in Architecture*, Peter Cook described the project as reminiscent of an airplane crash, which demonstrates, sadly, that he missed the whole point. By his metaphor, Cook reduced architecture once again to the status of a mere object, forcing it—crash!—into physical stasis by eliminating temporality and, together with temporality, all signs of life and utopian aspirations. This reading also separates the figure from its ground and therefore fails to appreciate the blurring—the *mise en* landscape—that is a critical element of the project.[14]

What Cook took as a mere representational act neglected completely the pathos in Giencke, or what Francis Bacon called "our obsession with life," which denies any possibility of irony and cynicism with such a thematic. Pathos and obsession are essential in this project, in its figurative moment, its relationship to landscape, and its concept of how human beings occupy space. Bacon's statement to an interviewer explains much about this ideology of the pathos of correspondence between life and art, which in his case found an emblem in the human body: "I think art is an obsession with life and after all, as we are human beings, our greatest obsession is with ourselves. Then possibly with animals, and then with landscapes."[15] In the same context,

Volker Giencke, drydock, Klagenfurt, 1982

Martin Häusle, pedestrian bridge, Feldkirch,
1987–1989

Volker Giencke, project for a high school, near Graz, 1982

Volker Giencke, botanical garden, Graz, 1982–1995, aerial photo of the site

when asked about his interest in landscape painting, Bacon replied: "Inability to do the figure." This resistance to figuration is a significant for understanding Giencke's obsession with landscape: architecture resists objecthood and becoming a mere figure against the landscape.

Giencke was not alone with his obsessions. Austrian art and architecture, especially after the 1960s, were very concerned with the body and with nature, which gained their most extreme expressions during the late 1960s in action painting and the *Wiener Aktionismus* (Viennese Actionism).[16] Giencke's obsession with life is manifested on different levels that resist formal analogy by making the obsession ultimately architectural, which is the event. When it comes to architecture, landscape is the last, but not the least, of the obsession's symptoms.

Judged by the use of new technology and inventive structural solutions, the glasshouses are easily labeled high-tech; yet on a closer look, the structural brilliance loses the status of being the main subject matter. Rather, everything appears as an image, evoking the picture of a wild, exotic garden—a paradise an earth—and a fantastic vision that prevents it from being reduced to the commonplace. The structure should be observed with this idea of suspension in mind.

The glasshouses are dominated by three transparent parabolic cylinders that penetrate one another diagonally, and an inclined glass roof that vanishes into the ground. The three parabolic cylinders serve as greenhouses open to the public, and contain arid, subtropical, and mild climate zones. The nurseries are located under the inclined roof. The rest of the built area, partly underground or otherwise less detectable, is reserved for service functions.

The supporting construction is made of hollow round tubes of aluminum alloy. The primary structure is made of two round, hollow parabolic arches, inclined in various degrees depending on the functional needs of each climatic zone (circulation, plant height), and the secondary structure is connected to the outer arches by cast aluminum joints. Both climate control and other installations are integrated into this carrying construction; the water-heating system is so integrated into the main construction that it acts like a huge radiator. The glazing is made of double-layered acrylic elements that wrap around the construction like a skin.

The visitor walks through the three main parts on ramps hung from the joints, descending and ascending through the areas. The inclination makes the spaces zoom either farther away or closer, depending on which way one perceives them.

Francis Bacon, *Two Figures on Grass,* 1954

Giencke's statement about the dynamics of *Gebaute Landschaft—Landschaft als Bauform* comes to full realization in this project, which also, for obvious programmatic motivation, becomes a laboratory for this thematic concern. Like movement, landscape provides a realm of temporality and change, and therefore becomes the area where the correspondence between humans and their environs is emphasized. The autonomy of the object becomes emblematic, as the clear figure-ground hierarchy, the Cook syndrome, is blurred. The glasshouses as such form an imaginary landscape that in turn contains a landscape: architecture *mise en* landscape or landscape *mise en* architecture.

The interiors of the three glasshouses form a landscape of artificial hills, steps, terraces, and walls. The concrete parts, combined with the forceful gestures of the retaining walls, partly made of random concrete slabs, add to the dialectics of the smooth picturesque framing as if the decline and transformation were already built into the landscape. The dynamic of a temporal landscape opposes again the stasis of traditional installations in botanical gardens. Nature is no more merely beautiful, but has the ability to balance with the dialectics of the picturesque and the sublime. The landscaping, which includes the buildings, combines smoothness and gentle curves with the boldness of the supporting construction. The combination is removed from the idealized concepts of landscape, but it manages to depict the very idea of landscape and nature within the real world and in real time.

This temporal feature of landscape and nature gives the project an ecological dimension that relies on this theory of presenting landscape not as an eternal flowing present or as stasis in a benign landscape but as dynamic processes that define a physical region. This relationship recalls the disposition behind the work of Robert Smithson and other land artists who opposed the ideology of nature as something natural and therefore eternal and unchangeable, promoted by those who believe in human control that excludes humans from nature.[17]

The glasshouses demonstrate the subtle dynamics that exist between architecture and nature when the former is conceived as built landscape. The landscape does not end at the borders of the interior space, but continues in the exterior space, blurring the borderline among natural nature, constructed landscape, and architecture. Yet the architecture does not mimic nature; it simply enhances the understanding of architecture and its impact on the land as raw material of the real. The building again manages to avoid simplifying the relationship that would reduce architecture to an effort to enhance the beauty of nature; instead, it participates in the relationship, becoming a paradigm of land manipulation devoid of both aggression toward and idealization of nature.

Peripheral Notions

Volker Giencke, botanical garden, general view of the site

Volker Giencke, botanical garden, view over the nursery toward the palm house

Right: Volker Giencke, botanical garden, close-up of the aluminum construction

Below, left: Volker Giencke, botanical garden, details of the aluminum construction

Below, right: Volker Giencke, botanical garden, interior view of the climate controlled house

Bottom, left: Volker Giencke, botanical garden, ground floor plan

Bottom, right: Volker Giencke, botanical garden, dividing wall in the palm house

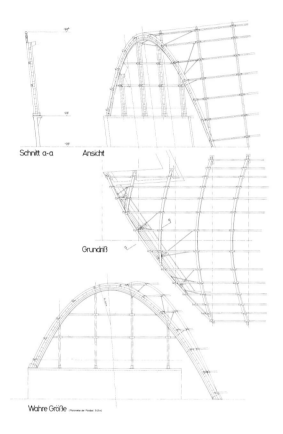

Schnitt a-a   Ansicht

Grundriß

Wahre Größe

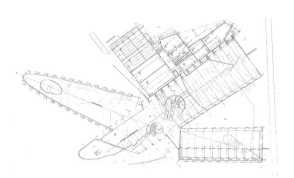

Francesco de Luca, installation for *Architecture
and Landscape* exhibition, Haus der Architektur,
Graz, 1991

Volker Giencke, botanical garden, model

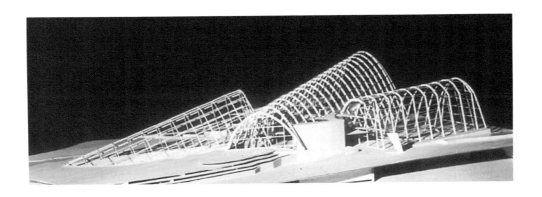

An interesting contribution to architecture *mise en* landscape was made in 1991 by Francesco de Luca, a member of a generation of architects younger than Giencke, as part of a seminar and exhibition called *Architektur und Landschaft* ("Architecture and Landscape") at the Haus der Architektur in Graz. De Luca wrapped the whole building in scaffolding carrying the name of the topic. The work demonstrated the obtrusive use of supplement in creating a double reversal: architecture disguises itself to achieve presence and blur simultaneously the figure-ground relationship by creating subtle boundaries. This obtrusive intervention bears a family resemblance to Giencke's Red Stage (de Luca worked with Giencke during the mid-1980s). Similarly, the wrapping implies temporality and potential uncovering; again the not-yet is embodied in the work. The permanent enclosure of the wall is replaced by a green and yellow fleece that covers the scaffolding. The scaffolding keeps architecture in a constant process of construction and transformation; the "more" lies in its incompletion and potentiality.

The installation for the Haus der Architektur is of interest because in it manifests the two possibilities of addressing landscape-architecture thematics. De Luca neglected to represent this relationship, which usually leads to endless speculation of how architecture has to relate vis-à-vis landscape, and instead chose to re-present the dialectic of becoming that exists between the two.

Anamorphosis Revisited

Cook's limited symbolic grasp of the botanical gardens seems especially hard to understand given the distortion produced by the manipulation of perspectival view. This distortion, which is emphasized by movement, makes it virtually impossible to perceive the work as the single figurative unity that Cook describes. These spatial effects were predicted by the model. And it is exactly the anamorphotic[18] aspect of the work that creates tension that by its very nature resists the figuration of the ground floor plan; this tension between figuration and distortion seems to be the critical basis for the whole work. The resistance to any single interpretation constantly blurs the hierarchy between figure and ground, and the simultaneous pull toward the creation of a certain figurative moment makes the work seductive. The gaze faces its limits; only movement and fantasy can extend it.

The glasshouses seem to be orchestrated for free drifting. Their critical potential is based on the view of existential space that belongs to the desiring, longing subject created through this drifting; the body is the domain where

Left: Constant, *Yellow Sector,* 1959

Opposite: Cedric Price, aviary at the London Zoo, 1961

Berthold Lubetkin and Lindsey Drake, penguin pool at the London Zoo, 1934

COOP Himmelblau, the Open House, Vienna, 1983

architecture becomes affective. The pledge that Deleuze makes for cinema has validity for architecture: "'Give me a body then': this is the formula of philosophical reversal. The body is no longer the obstacle that separates thought from itself, that which it has to overcome to reach thinking. It is on the contrary that which it plunges into or must plunge into, in order to reach the unthought, that is life. Not that the body thinks, but obstinate and stubborn, it forces us to think."[19] What is demanded from the arts is exactly to enhance the body as the paradigm of the social. Body is then no longer considered the prison of the soul, but that through which we relate to the world outside. Barthes puts it bluntly: "The pleasure of the text [architecture] is that moment when my body pursues its own ideas—for my body does not have the same ideas I do."[20]

The glasshouses celebrate and reassess the idea of *Großraum*, a model for spatial organization based on openness and programmatic flexibility. In this case a large open space is necessary for housing the plants, yet the idea is taken beyond the program by making the space for the garden, an oasis, into a wonderful playground. Giencke's glasshouses take the *Großraum* thematics beyond the conventional manipulation of a free plan that allows a flexible layout of programmatic requirements, while the space stretches the limits of the optimum structural solution and the contemporary technical requirements of housing botanical gardens. The structural and spatial idea of *Großraum*, when combined with wandering movement and destruction of simple perspectival reading, constructs room for play. It is revealing that during the planning process, government bureaucrats were worried about visitors becoming overexcited or rowdy on the hanging ramps. No more play!

Therefore the attraction of the *Großraum* lies more in the choreography and anticipation of chance enhanced by a nonprogrammatic plan being a model for the "communal, festive use of space," as Peter Wollen describes the spatial strategies of situationist architect Constant.[21] It allows for a psychogeography of space, the situationist *dérive*,[22] "a mode of experimental behavior linked to the conditions of urban society: a technique of transient passage through varied ambiances."[23] It is space that celebrates the accidental stroll that, although being mainly an urban attraction, can be transformed into desire embedded in architectural space. This principle resists the programmatic and functional, yet manages simultaneously to turn them into subject matter per se: function and movement become the event through their accidental, rather than predetermined and programmatic, unfolding. The visitor becomes the catalyst of that unfolding. The space is enacted by the simultaneous concealment and unconcealment of figure, function, form, and movement.

Wandering through the building, a viewer can perceive simultaneously a sequence of inside and outside spaces. Looking through the transparent acrylic glazing transforms the views into fictional scenery, the mere facts into something greater than life; like film, the work gains its quality from its ability to re-present life. Due to this blurring, one is constantly exposed to different happenings occurring simultaneously inside and outside the building. This manipulation of perception lets the architecture remain within the realm of the fantastic, so appropriate for a botanical garden. This touch of the unreal produces a desire for the real in fictional form. The real is indicated by the lack, which leads to the constant production of desire due to this very lack.

The creation of the fantastic, which in the glasshouses seems to be the main strategy for creating a space as an event, requires a radical, desiring subject. To maintain the enchantment, architecture faces the basic libidinal dilemma of how to go after something that can never be fully attained. In his discussion of psychoanalysis and cinema, Slavoj Žižek writes: "The paradox stages the relation of the subject to the object-cause of its desire, which can never be attained."[24] Anamorphosis gains its operational significance through the ability to hold a secret, erotic meaning, that is, the object-cause of desire in disguise. The power of the curious perspective is the act of participating in the production of that secret knowledge. Žižek continues: "Lacan's point is that the real purpose of the drive is not its goal (full satisfaction) but its aim: the drive's ultimate aim is simply to reproduce itself as drive, to return to its circular path, to continue its path to and from the goal. The real source of enjoyment is the repetitive movement of this closed circuit."[25] Architecture based on desire and event follows this libidinal economy, resisting the immediacy of experience that would provide the illusion of bliss, while reactivating desire by making it impossible to know or possess the work. The object must remain incomprehensible, fantastic, and therefore unattainable. Architecture is prevented thus from becoming "ready-at-hand" (Heidegger), simply an object.

The production of an event by manipulating movement to achieve the endless unfolding of an object is a prime example of desire based on the dynamic relationship between subject and object. The botanical garden can be perceived as a materialization of the distortion that produces desire as the "surplus of confusion" (Žižek). The unreal and fantastic quality of the work is based on the way things really appear to us; the distorted dimensions (zooming) and the fact that the building can never be perceived as a whole make it appear almost hallucinatory.

Right: Volker Giencke, botanical garden, interior view of the palm house showing the bridge

Middle: J. -F. Niceron, *Anamorphose conique de Louis XIII,* 1638

Bottom left: Volker Giencke, botanical garden the palm house under construction, the zooming effect

Bottom right: Volker Giencke, botanical garden, section of the subtropic house

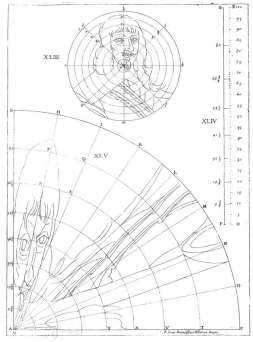

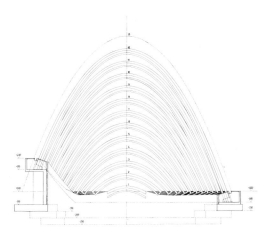

Gordon Matta Clark, *Caribbean Orange* series,
1934

The work does not simply represent desire, a shortcoming of works using a more expressive formal vocabulary. Rather, desire is a constituent of a constantly changing evanescent set of scenes that take on the character of fictional or virtual space as we move through them. It is exactly this opposition to representation and the transformation of the real into fiction that make desire possible.

Virtuality is produced by movement along the hanging ramps; the perceiver is taken for a ride with, but partly distanced from, the architecture. Architecture exists both within and without the temporal and spatial situation. Semibelonging allows the work to retain both its fantastic and magical (garden) qualities, and therefore it cannot provide a fully absorbing spatial experience. It is always at a distance, as if observed from outside, stimulating the visitor's desire to be within and become part of the paradise.

Desire is a response to (un)attainable fulfillment. The construction of desire is based on the construction of lack: "The fundamental point of psychoanalysis is that desire is not something given in advance, but something that has to be constructed—and it is precisely the role of fantasy to give the coordinates of the subject's desire, to specify its object, to locate the position the subject assumes in it. It is only through fantasy that the subject is constituted as desiring: *through fantasy, we learn how to desire.*" [26] The fictional in the botanical garden is based on this element of the unreal and fantastic embedded in its visionary character, and is hard to dismiss even when looking only at drawings or the model.

The lack of the real is constructed through the constant fluctuation between contracting and expanding space; inclined parabolic forms establish a false perspective that changes as we move in different directions. The work is ungraspable: no matter from what angle we perceive it, the whole remains unclear. It is anamorphotic and does not allow one straight, disinterested, or objective look. To experience the work, we must "look awry," as Žižek characterizes the anamorphotic experience. He writes:

If we look at a thing straight on, matter-of-factly, we see it "as it really is," while the gaze puzzled by our desires and anxieties ("looking awry") gives us a distorted, blurred image. On the level of the second metaphor, however, the relationship is the opposite: if we look at a thing straight on, i.e., matter-of-factly, disinterestedly, objectively, we see nothing but a formless spot; the object assumes clear and distinctive features only if we look at it "at an angle," i.e., with an "interested" view, supported, permeated, and "distorted" by desire. This describes perfectly the objet petit a, the object-cause of desire: an object that is, in a way, posited by desire itself. The paradox of desire is that it posits retroactively its own cause, i.e., the object a is an object that can be perceived only by a gaze

1970s in Berlin through the major work by Hans Scharoun, and in Finland by Reima Pietilä, for whom it provided access to the unexplored territories of modern architecture, to its intermediate zones.

Graz joined this tradition most notably with the work of Günther Domenig. His multipurpose hall in Graz Eggenberg is a sprayed concrete shell in a form that looks somewhat like a dragon. It dates from late 1970s and marks the beginning of an oeuvre that is dominated by a highly individualistic language tied to different figurative analogues of natural forms. A number of his disciples followed, with various emphases, the path opened by Domenig's exuberant architectural language, most notably Michael Szyszkowitz and Karla Kowalski with their anthropomorphic structures reminiscent of Rudolf Steiner's Goetheum in Steinach: heavy and earthbound. Some others, such as Klaus Kada, since the late 1970s have rejected the organic vocabulary altogether. Domenig's recent work seems to move toward the sculptural, manifesting the influence of Walter Pichler and Carlo Scarpa, and his metaphors have become increasingly enigmatic and mystical. In Steinhaus, a house that Domenig has been building for himself for the past ten years, metaphors of childhood (site) and death (the abyss) take on a Freudian twist.

Among the architects with penchant for the organic, a group that came to be known as the *Grazer Schule* after a group exhibition that took place in 1981, Giencke is perhaps the most subtle in his use of the organic and less committed to this single architectural language. In his case we should not think of the organic as being an individualized gesture. His work joins the peripheral tendencies of the modern by uniting with the tradition set by Aalto, Scharoun, Häring, and Pietilä in the twentieth century. Yet, rather than merely affirming this tradition, Giencke's appropriation of the organic adds to it by being essentially antiformal. The organic line celebrates disclosure and figurative ambiguity; the turn to the organic reverses and challenges the form: Once the organic has been discovered and serves as a point of departure, it really does not matter any more. This attitude clearly separates his work also from that of the other members of the *Grazer Schule*.

The new use of the organic line that makes its appearance in architecture after the 1960s must therefore be placed in a different contextual framework than that of Aalto, Mendelson, or even Scharoun and Häring. It is no longer the romantic or expressionist line, but a line of sublation and doubting, as well as one that challenges form altogether—the line of desire.

These other conceptions of the organic line go beyond the figurative, beyond the merely intuitive individual gesture. A different sort of organic supports the idea of architecture as a process. The fact that architecture no longer starts by imposing any single form as an overall organization deriving

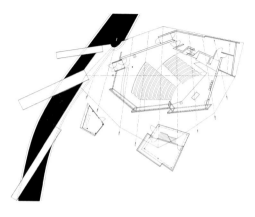

Top: Volker Giencke, parish church, ground floor plan

Volker Giencke, parish church, Aigen, Ennstal, 1985–1992 (photo: Paul Ott)

Top, left: Günther Domenig, multipurpose hall, Graz-Eggenberg, 1974–1977

Top, right: Günther Domenig, multipurpose hall, interior

Bottom, left: Michael Szyszkowitz and Karla Kowalski, castle renovation, Großlobming, 1981

Bottom, right: Klaus Kada, Sparkasse, Bad Radkersburg, 1977–1980

Right: Günther Domenig, Steinhaus, sketch

Günther Domenig, Steinhaus, 1986

Bottom: Michael Szyszkowitz and Karla Kowalski,
experimental housing, Stuttgart, 1989–1993

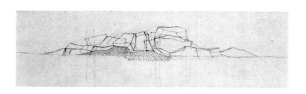

Hugo Häring, Gargau farm, 1927

from outside is represented by this line. The organic form is one of constant aberration. The organic creates "a fictionalized, symbolic code instead of abstraction,"[33] as Roger Connah observes, focusing on the dichotomy in twentieth-century architecture between the production of a symbolic and figurative code and the ideology of abstraction.

To relocate the organic, one must consider the difference between figuration and representation. There is a lot of confusion about this. The organic does not represent nature or the human body. It figures nature only in the sense that it participates in the temporality and transformability that are inseparable from nature. Indeed, it is a way of escaping the representation innate in abstraction. We might join Barthes in understanding representation as a "space of alibis" such as reality, morality, and truth. Architecture, which allows the possibility of figuration as an organic line, seems to be haunted by life as a sensual fact. Therefore, rather than trying to depict the essence of the real through representation, which forces everything into a frame, the figurative has a more direct contact with the real.

The church in Aigen is the most organic in Giencke's oeuvre. The dominating element of the building is the inclined roof, built in a kitelike form constructed like a ship whose middle axis lies parallel to the nave. The roof is covered with grass and it cantilevers over the church proper, leaving the supporting iron beams to reach some 5 meters beyond the wall. One of the supports even lands in the brook that lies at the edge of the site, a gesture important for defining the relationship with the landscape. The church consists of three separate buildings: the church proper in an irregular polygonal shape, the bell tower, and the vicarage; the last two were conceived as distorted rectangles in the plan.

The building combines concrete, wood, steel, and glass in ways such that the materials have the ability to go beyond simple structural logic. Glass, for example, is found in the most unpredictable place of all: as the siding for the church tower. Giencke seems to be most attached to photographic images that depict the glass tower from a distance in a foggy Ennstal landscape; the vertical of the transparent tower is hardly visible, yet it seems to create an axis in the middle of the valley.

Whereas the sculptural too often relies on a particular kind of emotional response evoked by abstract representations of spirituality and immortality, the organic is opposed to such transcendental aesthetics. The figurative stays within the sphere of mortals. The abstract, sculptural form wanting to represent the eternal is a perfect metaphor for representation in general: once again a frame—a time frame, time stopped. "That is what representation is: when

Hans Scharoun, Philharmonic Concert Hall, main
auditorium

Hans Scharoun, Philharmonic Concert Hall,
Berlin, 1956–1963, ground floor plan

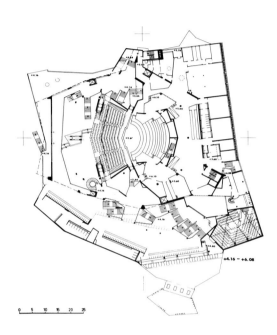

nothing emerges, when nothing leaps out of the frame; of the picture, the book, the screen." [34] The sculptural has a particular kind of silence that always stays within the frame.

The selection of the organic language, especially for a church, was likely motivated by the potential symbolic and existential code embedded in the doubting line. The fact that the church in Aigen seems to bear a distant formal relationship to Le Corbusier's Ronchamp Chapel comes as no surprise. Many motifs stem from a close study of Corbusier's subtle use of symbols: the unfinished red wall emphasizes that the church is finally a common process of building a community, while it recalls the wall of blood in Ronchamp. A more distant relationship can be found between Giencke's use of the stained glass wall and the orchestration of light through the irregular window openings in Corbusier's church. In both cases the symbolic stresses the existential and the communal dimensions of the Christian church.

The insinuating and nervous line of the organic cannot be reduced to an individual gesture, trying to challenge the universal geometric grid, as Frampton suggested. This diminishes the organic to unresolved dichotomies between universal and particular, or alternatively, following Freud, between pleasure

Volker Giencke, parish church, ground floor plan
and section of the bell tower

Volker Giencke, parish church, longitudinal section through the church proper

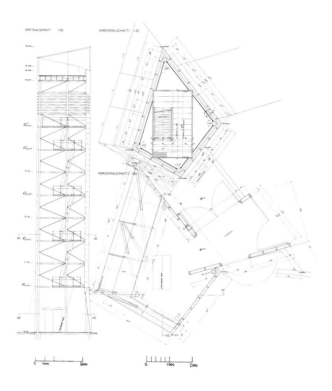

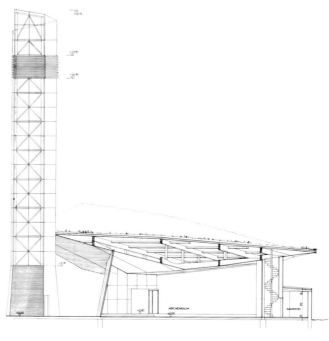

and reality principles; in both cases the particular and pleasure will always be doomed finally to play second fiddle. The organic line defines a third domain that cannot be located in either the universal order or in deliverance from that order. Marcuse's critique of the Freudian pleasure principle could be expanded to cover the reduction of the organic to individual gesture: "Liberation follows domination—and leads to reaffirmation of domination."[35]

To discuss the organic we must reassess the relationship between the straight line and the suggestive undulating line. Ernst Bloch's discussion of human and animal principles makes us question the dominance of rationality and its best emblem, the straight line, as the most predominant characteristics of human nature. Bloch writes: "The orgy distinguishes man from animals, more clearly than reason; man does not stop when he has enough."[36] His principle of the orgy, or the carnival if you wish, challenges the dominant motive of twentieth-century architectural modernism captured by Le Corbusier's early dictum of "the pack-donkey's way and man's way,"[37] wherein he considers human acts as something determined solely by the economy of means and rational establishment of a goal, as opposed to the arbitrariness of animal actions. Bloch's sentence and his fellow critical thinkers rewrite modernity by linking it to the will to excess rather than to the economy of reason. Compared with the dominant ideology of twentieth-century architecture, that of the straight line and the right angle, the suggestive sinuous line reminds us of the superficial dichotomies that our thinking is based on: universal versus particular, economy versus superfluousness, and finally, art versus reality, by demonstrating the mechanism of production that forces us to remain in the seam.

The most evident gesture of the organic lies in its exaggeration. Behind excess and exaggeration lie the indecisiveness and nervousness that characterize desire, which can become endlessly prolonged through the work's open-endedness. The seduction of the organic is based on this disclosure, which turns the organic into a method of production rather than of representation. Roger Connah discusses the process behind the organic through the work of Pietilä, which led the organic architecture of the post-Aalto era beyond the strategies of a grid opposed to a free, individual gesture: ". . . composition [is to be understood] as a malleable, unending process, and the subsequent transformation even of that process itself. *The open work*. The *composer* then of the emerging form and the *performer* of that form, indeterminate, to close and open, to remain referential and abstract."[38] Pietilä replies: "The mobility of components makes modification possible. The process of transformation and composition is concentrated and the existing interrelations easily perceptible.

Volker Giencke, parish church, view of Aigen and
the bell tower (photo: Paul Ott)

Volker Giencke, parish church, view toward the
bell tower showing the vicarage on the left,
church proper on the right (photo: Paul Ott)

Volker Giencke, parish church, interior view toward the altar (photo: Paul Ott)

Volker Giencke, law school for the University of Graz, competition project, 1985, structural model

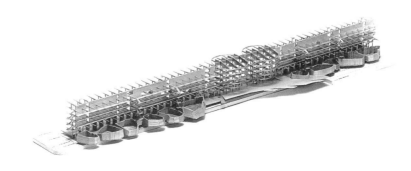

Below: Reima Pietilä and Raili Paatelainen, Dipoli student center, Espoo, 1966 (photo: Martti I. Jaatinen)

Middle, left: Reima Pietilä and Raili Paatelainen, Dipoli, ground floor plan

Middle, right: Reima Pietilä and Raili Paatelainen, Dipoli, the main hall (photo: Martti I. Jaatinen)

Bottom: Volker Giencke, law school project, sketch of the auditoriums

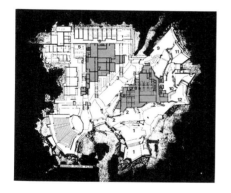

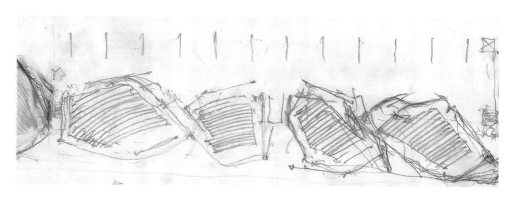

The composition is also modified by light—itself a transformer."[39] The end-less modifications come to demonstrate the process of the form of form. Form is here understood as an operational move rather than as a end in itself.

There is a seduction in this incompletion: "vacillation—I stumble, I err. In any case there will always be a margin of indecision; the distinction will not be the source of absolute classifications, the paradigm will falter, the meaning will be precarious, revocable, reversible, the discourse *incomplete*,"[40] as Barthes describes the indescribable of the "pleasure of the text." The or-ganic shares the strategies of poststructuralist ideas of text and can be experi-enced only in an activity of production; the line can never stop. Barthes posits the difference between the two by defining the text as essentially a "method-ological field" that "goes to the limit of the rules of enunciation (rationality, readability)."[41] By defining the text as a strategy, he aims to locate what he calls the "subversity edge." Barthesian cultural politics returns us to Adorno: the text looks for the seam, for the liminal zone between a simultaneous ne-gation and acceptance of some cultural code. Barthes writes: "Culture thus recurs as an edge: in no matter what."[42] The organic must be understood as a zone, a threshold between inside and outside, revealing and concealing, "the staging of an appearance-as-disappearance,"[43] that is, the ultimate erotic. The desire is constantly prolonged and *en attendance*, awaiting the unfolding. The organic always evolves and unfolds within temporality.

Architectural historian Jürgen Joedicke considers this open-endedness as a lack of method and as the main reason why the organic principle failed to lead architectural discourse in the twentieth century. This only supports the dominant culture and fails to understand the importance of such questioning undercurrents in society. Such undercurrents provide an epistemological break in the tradition of architecture by disinterest in the question of how to define architecture. Richard Rorty makes the same point: "Edifying philoso-phers can never end philosophy, but they can help prevent it from attaining a secure path of science."[44]

The Glaze: Phantasm and Modern Architecture

The demand for ambiguity and the fictional seems to be a common domi-nator in all the operational moves discussed in this chapter. It gains its ulti-mate expression in glass, which has dominated modern architecture ever since the erection of the Crystal Palace for the 1851 world exhibition. Glass has become a mythic trope for the subject matter of modern architecture: technology, openness, harmony with nature. The typical building types that were born with glass architecture—the glasshouse, the railway station, the

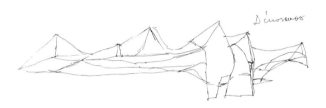

Reima Pietilä: Dinosaurus sketch for Dipoli

exhibition hall, the gallery—are also sites for the ultimate modern experience: the urban stroll, the *dérive*, a moment when we willingly surrender ourselves to the sensuous stimulus that enters our consciousness without control, and the most urban experience of all, the seductive opportunity to look and be looked at. Early glass architecture was meant for transient purposes, for acts experienced by the masses, rather than as places for individual contemplation. It created scenes of desire, power, and collective experience.[45]

Glass also takes architecture back to the early modern era by emphasizing spiritual, visual, and social qualities. According to Scheerbart, it brings a completely new mode of life into being. He reveals his spiritual motivation: "Glass architecture makes homes into cathedrals, with the same effects."[46] Glass also was to represent the shock of the new, having an almost hypnotizing power over the spectator. Underlying its use was the will for change, change that could not be preprogrammed in terms of a definite goal. The elusiveness of glass and its ability to enter into a reciprocal relationship with its environment by means of light became the perfect symbol for change and the new, still devoid of any singular meaning.

Glass architecture has gone through many phases since Paxton's Crystal Palace. It began with glasshouses, and orangeries that were conceived as arenas for fantastic and exotic gathered from all over the world. Therefore its origins were in travel, commodity fetishism, and the longing for paradise, which had as their source the desire for the new and fantastic. All that changed in the late 1920s.

Twentieth-century mainstream modernism found glass attractive for quite different reasons. It emphasized either the romantic and sentimental belief in the continuity between humans and nature with the flow of spaces between the inside and outside of a building, or the pragmatic advantages of maximum penetration of light in terms of hygiene.[47] It reduced glass to a mere transparent material, something one sees through. Yet it is the mythic in the early modern tradition that serves as a point of reference for contemporary architects who seem obsessed by glass as an embodiment of the subtle complexities of their poetic and symbolic language.

Glass is the emblem of the modern in the sense that it amalgamates even opposites into a symbolic unity. Hugo von Hofmannstahl's description of the experience at the turn of the last century seems appropriate: "Today, two things seem to be modern: the analysis of life and the flight from life . . . One practises anatomy on the inner life of one's mind, or one dreams. Reflection or fantasy, mirror image or dream image."[48] As discussed by James McFarlane, the modern is understood as a combination of two *Weltanschauungen*: the mech-

Top, left: Bruno Taut, *Alpine Architecture,* 1918

Top, right: Volker Giencke, Odörfer showroom and warehouse, Klagenfurt, 1991, reflections on the warehouse wall

Bottom: Ludwig Mies van der Rohe, project for a glass skyscraper, Berlin,1922, model

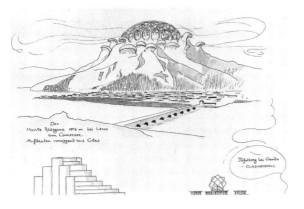

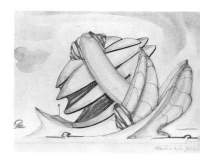

Hermann Finsterlin, *Dream of Glass,* aquarel,
1920

anistic and the intuitive. Hofmannstahl notes that "modern" at the turn of
the century meant a coalescence and fusion of dream and reality to the point
of indistinguishability. For him as well as for Simmel[49] and other contemporaries it meant that humans had partly lost control over the stimuli produced
by technology and life in a metropolis. To lose control and to deal with ambiguities and discontinuities became part of the modern experience; therefore, fragment and the particular gain importance over abstraction and the
generalization.

By virtue of its elusive materiality glass can blur the line between nature
and technology, between inside and outside, between the real and the imaginary. It plays with notions of the ephemeral and the permanent, as well as
with those of the real and the imaginary. By adding to the real a quality of
the imaginary, and to the imagined a possibility of transformation into the
real, what was considered permanent becomes transient. Glass rotates images
between the two, adding an ephemeral quality to real objects and places
and obscuring the real and turning it into a dream vision. Its inherent
qualities are wish and potentiality. Glass is an antonym for ruin: it means
not-yet, whereas ruin implies no-more. By enacting a wish, it suggests
transformation.[50]

Adding Taut's and Scheerbart's visionary glass utopias to our discussion,
it seems that early glass architecture always aimed at exceeding mere architecture; it attempted to change life by constituting new realities. There is something magical about the space of glass that produces moments of self-
transcendence understood as typically modern, and urban experience per se.
Glass has two main qualities that support this idea of something greater than
reality-yet-present. First, as Benjamin noted, it is the enemy of recollections
and possessions because it is perpetually new, and second, due to its obvious
tie to modern technology, glass architecture always promises to create something not-yet-present (Bloch). Conceived as such it becomes the emblem of
what Walter Benjamin calls a wish-image. In disguise, overtly present through
reflection, or transparent, which is its most harmonious of incarnations, glass
always seems to play with perceivers by manipulating what we consider real.

The return to the beginning of modern (glass) architecture of the mid-
nineteenth century can be explained by the fact that utopian images, which
are always accompanied by the emergence of the new, reach back to the Ur-
past, as Susan Buck-Morss discusses in her study of Benjamin's *Passagenwerke.*
Thus it returns to its origin, as enlightenment visionaries turned to the *Urhütte.*
This reflection makes the contemporary mythic through the tradition it follows, and it is exactly the mythic and symbolic quality that activates the uto-

Wassili Luckhardt, *Crystal,* ca. 1920

pian impulse. Contemporary glass architecture reassesses the myth of the modern by recalling its own tradition.[51]

The utopian impulse relies on the ability of glass architecture to appropriate the relationship between architecture and technology. Through technology, architecture participates in industrial production, which constantly transforms reality. As Benjamin discussed in his famous article "Art in the Age of Mechanical Reproduction," only by using new methods of production can art have an impact on the masses, albeit also an alarming impact. Through the symbolic liaison between technology and nature, art anticipates the production and change of reality that only technology seems to have mastered. Glass architecture participates in this production of reality by means of a shock that, quoting Giorgio Agamben, "appropriates unreality."[52] Agamben thus refers to the late nineteenth-century ideas of modernity in his discussion about the reassessment of art in the era of industrial revolution. Recalling Benjamin, he writes:

Baudelaire understood that if art wished to survive industrial civilization, the artist had to attempt to reproduce that destruction of use-value and traditional intelligibility that was at the origin of the experience of shock. In this way the artist would succeed in making the work the vehicle of the unattainable and would restore in unattainability itself a new value and a new authority. . . . Without the personal experience of the miraculous ability of the fetish object to make the absence present through its own negation, he would perhaps not have dared to assign to art the most ambitious task that any human being has ever entrusted to one of his or her creations: the appropriation of unreality.[53]

There are countless examples of the use of glass in contemporary European architecture, yet few demonstrate the sensibilities that make it perhaps the most powerful fiction of modernity. The excessive use of glass in Giencke's showroom and warehouse in Klagenfurt reveals some of the ideas that address the quintessentially modern sensibilities that the material engages. It is the ambiguity of the material, its malleability, its changing incarnations that become the subject matter.

Commissioned by the firm Odörfer, and often referred to as such, the building occupies a site by the ring road through the industrial zone near Klagenfurt. It is dominated by a 65-m-long tilted glass roof; or maybe it is more appropriate to define it as a wall that has become a roof. This roof-wall rises from the ground at a slight angle. The ambiguous relationship between building and ground demonstrates that the building wants to be more than a mere inanimate object; it wants to become part of the real by raising itself

Volker Giencke, Odörfer, long elevation showing
showroom on the left, office-bar in the middle,
and warehouse on the right

Volker Giencke, Odörfer, glass roof over
the showroom

from the ground, simulating animation by the combination of a wall turning into a roof and back into a wall when viewed in motion, and by the way glass changes character in this situation. Our attention is drawn first of all to this fragment from which the building later unfolds. The eye seems to stay on the surface rather than look through. "Like all desire, vision should be conceived from the beginning in relation to lack, a drift from metaphor to metaphor, an infinite chain of difference."[54] The showroom becomes vaguely visible when the roof is seen at a right angle.

The long glass surface is parallel to the road, and sometimes in late summer it is almost invisible from farther than a few hundred meters away due to the high cornfield that surrounds the site. The uncanniness of the roof is due to its sudden appearance. Seeing is not simultaneous with recognition: viewed sideways, the roof reflects the sky melting into it to the point of absolute disappearance. A few seconds later one grasps the physical reality and presence of the building. At first one imagines a totally different material for the roof. Only later, when the reflection turns it transparent, does the surface reveal its materiality. This happens when one is level with the building and the roof starts suddenly to change both its form and incarnation: the tilted reflective or opaque (depending on the light) surface suddenly becomes a semitransparent wall. It is hardly surprising that the glass roof almost caused a few car accidents; we actually thought about erecting a traffic sign with the text "*Achtung Architektur!*" One becomes aware of the building at the moment when the reflection becomes transparent. Having given us no chance of visual control and adjustment, the building's presence comes as an absolute surprise.

The second level of confrontation happens afterward when perception has yielded to an after-image, a dreamlike vision that allows an allegorical reading. It is this prolongation of the actual confrontation by means of the image that stays with the perceiver and exceeds what might otherwise be an isolated experience. The image again looks for the material emblem of the "involuntary beauty of the ephemeral"[55]—the veil. The use of glass in Odörfer reminds me of Christo's wrappings, which also rely on the singularity of instant confrontation. The unreal quality of the glass surface, at first opaque and reflecting, then transparent, similarly suggests an act of unfolding, unveiling.

Most critics still talk about architecture's will for disappearance, transparency, and dematerialization. I suggest it is the ability of glass to transform itself into three incarnations, the transparent, opaque, and reflecting, while remembering the moments of transformation in between, that reveals its am-

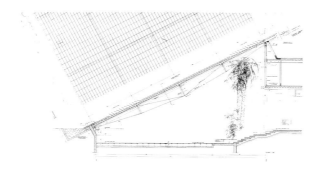

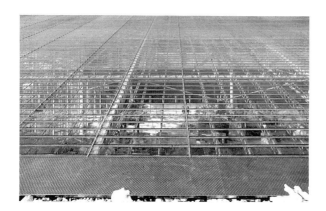

biguous quality. The element of surprise, the game of hide and seek, and the metamorphosis from one incarnation to another make the discovery of boundary, of material surface, an arrival. Conceived as such, glass seems to be as much about appearance and materialization—unfolding—as it is about disappearance and dematerialization. Architecture devoid of metaphysics turns into an object of desire that has its own animated presence. Glass's gaze (glaze) explains something about the will "to deprive the external world of the privilege of being inanimate." [56] The animation is based on the ability of glass to react to changes of light conditions as well as to the position of the spectator. Reflection and opacity conceal and force the eye to wander in search of revelation and arrival, whereas the transparent condition embodies the final bliss by revealing the materiality of glass, and allowing the spectator to know the interior.

A curtain and a mirror play with the idea of simultaneous concealing and revealing. Glass reveals something before it is available and tangible, sustains things as objects of desire that are not yet there to be possessed or, in the case of architecture, spaces not yet accessible. In Odörfer the tease reaches its climax when the glass louvers of the roof open: the ultimate exhibitionist act. This ability to move and to react to outer stimuli defines the skin of Odörfer as an "osmotic membrane," a zone of "transference between two milieus, two substances" that Paul Virilio talks about—an invisible difference. [57]

Glass architecture has traditionally been employed to emphasize different aspects, mainly continuity and vastness, as the conceptions of modern architectural space. Contemporary glass architecture, on the contrary, seems to prove the impossibility (even immorality) of representing space as a hierarchically defined structure. Examples demonstrate this by emphasizing the ambiguity, not elimination, of the boundary of space. The veiling turns spatiality into temporality, the most subjective element of human experience according to Merleau-Ponty. The process of unveiling makes time into both a visual and a sensuous element.

Top: Volker Giencke, Odörfer, night view of the
glass roof

Middle: Helmut Richter, high school, Vienna,
1991–1994, view from southwest

Bottom: Hermut Richter, high school, gymnastic
hall, interior

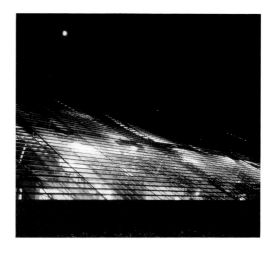

Toward the Aesthetics
of the Incomplete

. . . All art is erotic.
The first ornament that was born, the cross, was erotic in origin.
The first work of art, the first artistic act which the first artist, in
order to rid himself of his surplus energy, smeared on the wall. A
horizontal dash: the prone woman. A vertical dash: the man penetrating her. The man who created it felt the same urge as
Beethoven, he was in the same heaven in which Beethoven created
the Ninth Symphony.

—**Adolf Loos**

Ornament Today

If architecture is to resist mere objecthood and gain the quality of something taking place, the question arises, how are we to understand such resistance? We can to a certain degree agree with COOP Himmelblau's demand for architecture to burn and to have more. It is the excess (the more) and the ambiguity (the flame) that constitute the energy required for change; excess guarantees continuing transformation through perpetual incompletion. In their demands, needless to say, COOP Himmelblau stays faithful to their revolutionary 1960s stance and rhetoric.[2]

Adolf Loos was an early compatriot of Wolfgang Prix and Helmut Swiczinsky. Unlike the latter, Loos was suspicious of all excess and was more specific in locating the energy that makes the work tremble. Ornament for him was an emblem of all excess and impurity, which threaten the values of the modern capitalist society. It is interesting to compare Loos's "Ornament and Crime," published in 1908, with COOP Himmelblau's "Architecture Must Burn," published in 1980, not only because all of the writers are Viennese, but also because of their antithetical stances. To put it bluntly, the latter liked everything Loos detested and despised.

Loos's intention was to control the energy and desire embodied in ornament; for him it represented the body's sexual energy that has to be suppressed and sublimated. Prix and Swiczinsky, on the other hand, faithful to their antiauthoritarian stance in favor of sexual freedom, insist that architecture can trigger that desire. Loos must have been aware of this ability of space to awaken desire, so telling were his insights.

Loos came up with a strategy. Rather than eliminate ornament and those aspects of life associated with it, he wanted to control the energy inherent in ornament by turning it inward and channeling it into making art. Art for art's sake became the realm of sublimation and a controlled outlet for an individual's energy surplus; thus it was the only kind of surplus that modern society could afford to produce and enjoy in a civilized, nondestructive manner.

BEUYS

For COOP Himmelblau such separation of art and architecture that attempts to locate and control the surplus hardly exists. In their work surplus becomes the main subject matter, so that finally one cannot even distinguish where it begins and utility ends: ornament takes over. Architecture refuses to be merely useful and economical, and begins to challenge its traditional place, limitations, and modes of representation. The main question of twentieth-century art, what is art?, is followed by the question, what is architecture?

Ornament and excess are important to consider because they introduce questions of economy, morality, and politics into architectural discourse. These lead to the assessment of values and rules (the police) through the manipulation of symbolic codes. What constitutes excess often bears the stigma of

Top, right: Louis Sullivan, Teller's wicket, National Farmers' Bank, (photo: John Gronkowski photography) Owatonna, Minnesota, 1906–1908

Bottom, left: Book of Kells, the beginning of St. Mark's gospel

impurity (the crime) by preserving something of the actual act of making. A work born from excess can be understood as a trace. Due to its character as a trace, ornament seems to Loos impure because it does not respect the boundary between art and utilitarian objects. This failure challenges the economic imperative of the society confronting it with the psychological values and needs of the individual. Art should serve the latter, and utilitarian objects, to which Loos assigns most architecture, should be restricted to serve the former.

Ornament is also impure because it does not mediate meaning and it cannot be understood as an immediate sensuous presence. Rather, like hieroglyphs, it keeps vacillating between apparent clarity and decipherability and the obscure. Always on the verge of blurring the figure-ground hierarchy, it makes it difficult or even impossible to tell one from the other: excess takes over. Using Nietzsche's terminology, we can say that ornament leads us to consider two opposed world views: the Apollonian sphere where "nothing is in excess" and the Dionysian sphere where "excess reveals itself as truth."[3]

The economic imperative supports a more or less stable value system: money. Underlying it is the assumption that a free market best serves a state that is wanted by all—total consensus. Loos therefore thought he was supported by obvious moral values and was working toward a better society when he proclaimed, "We have outgrown ornament; we have fought our way through to freedom from ornament. See, time is right, fulfillment awaits us. Soon the street of the city will glisten like white walls. Like Zion, the holy city, the capital of heaven."[4] Whiteness represents the elimination of excess, which becomes an act of moral hygiene. All real change includes conflict and excess; because he eliminates both, Loos is left with no more than a promise of change. A world based on utilitarian values can exist only in a vacuum between original sin and the promised fulfillment. Loos's aesthetic is based on a myth that conflates Christian hopes and dreams of economic evolution. This myth requires eliminating from the world the excess of primal energy inherent in pure matter. It also requires eliminating the friction between art and society by the mystification of art. Thus art is turned into a commodity.

Whether we welcome it or not, we have to admit that, in this dichotomy, excess holds the key to possible transformation and change. When human artifacts are rid of internal and external conflicts, mystification inevitably supports the status quo devoid of any possibility of change. As Adorno observes, "The state free of ornament would be a utopia of concretely fulfilled presence . . ."[5]; form and content, symbol and meaning would become one, and there would be no place for obscurity and change.

Like Loos, but for different reasons, Adorno and Bloch view ornament in a manner that combines physical and mental visions associated with the body. But whereas the sensuous and sexual connotations of ornament horrified Loos, for the very same reason Adorno and Bloch find ornament appealing. It is a perfect metaphor for the body, understood as a site for the overlapping of the private and the public, that is, of politics.[6] Loos is disgusted by "the tortured, strained, and morbid quality of modern ornaments,"[7] which combine personal, social, and political connotations within a single physical image. This was the same quality that was to be celebrated by such post-Marxist thinkers as Lefebvre, who valued "spatial practice" as a directly lived experience over its conceptualization.[8] The elimination of ornament was therefore a precondition for sustaining the direct correspondence between form and idea; human activity or the traces of the actual making process should play no role in the final work. This quality of ornament presented a threat to Loos. Adorno and Bloch welcomed the ability of ornament to merge different levels of meaning and associations into one image because it breaks the inner coherence and isolation of the work. Therefore to Bloch, ornament functions as a mediator among art work, reality, and memory. For Loos, it is a metonym for desire: bodily metaphors express ornament's political significance.

COOP Himmelblau joins in the criticism of Loos's pro-status quo stance. Earlier critics singled out ornament as a metonym for the hopes and desires that modernism left unfulfilled. Adorno thus is in opposition to Loos mainly because of his anticipation of a controversial relationship between culture and society; rather than advocating culture to bring order to chaos, Adorno argues the opposite. Loos's metaphysical and antidialectical aesthetics were based on eliminating the problem of form, which is based on the interaction between subject and matter. The status quo was supported by passive subjectivity, which dominates Loos' idea of the design process.[9] Like many of his fellow modernists he believed in the idea of a constitutive zeitgeist; following Hegel, he failed to recognize the active role of the subject, while believing in a harmonious outcome of will and idea in human creations.

For the opposing camp of Marxist critics the constitutive agency of the subject gains importance. Exactly in the act of making and in active imagination the subject can experience a moment of nonalienation. As Loos describes in his example of the cross, ornament suspends the memory of the actual act: the dash. In the following passage Adorno compresses and materializes his dialectical aesthetics by integrating making and imagining, form and thought. He presents us with another type of creative agent that, opposed to Loos's passive subject, is laden with consciousness and desire. Consciousness and desire merge with the material. This artistic imagination discovers new if ineffable potential within the real.

Clearly there exists, perhaps imperceptible in the materials and forms which the artist acquires and develops something more than material and forms. Imagination means to innervate this something. This is not as absurd a notion as it may sound. For the forms, even the materials, are by no means merely given by nature, as an unreflective artist might easily presume. History has accumulated in them, and spirit permeates them. What they contain is not a positive law; and yet, their content emerges as a sharply outlined figure of the problem. Artistic imagination awakens these accumulated elements by becoming aware of the innate problematic of the material. The minimal progress of imagination responds to the wordless question posed to it by the material and forms in their quiet and elemental language. Separate impulses, even purpose and immanent formal laws, are thereby fused together. An interaction takes place between purpose, space, and material. None of these facets makes up any one Ur-phenomenon to which all the others can be reduced. It is here that the insight furnished by philosophy that no thought can lead to an absolute beginning—that such absolutes are the products of abstraction—exerts its influence on aesthetics.[10]

The eternal question between self-expression and order, between individual and community, also culminate in ornament. The balance achieved between the individual gesture (the famous Aalto line) and universal order (the grid), what Kenneth Frampton later labeled as critical regionalism, hardly describes the way ornament operates.[11] Instead of cooperating in this way, ornament, unlike the compositional undulating line of Utzon and Aalto, disconnects with its ground and revolts against it. Due to its own productive systems—rotation, symmetry, repetition—it resists total submission to any underlying order. Louis Sullivan's ornaments are the best examples of this resistance: ornament is essentially a confrontational element that keeps the work from settling into any hierarchical system.

It is exactly this aspect of ornament that makes it important for the relocation of architecture as building in contemporary society: the rediscovery of the act of making architecture, a rediscovery that goes beyond the idea of mere self-expression based on the illusion that both subject and object exist in a vacuum. I would like to test the idea that the self-production of ornament can lead to the relocation of both the subject and the object outside themselves giving architecture a potentially critical role in modern society, a role based primarily on the reassessment of the act of making itself. This reassessment of the making process questions form as a primal carrier of meaning by integrating new concepts, for example, those of temporality and materiality, into thinking and imagining architecture and its level of meaning. I also maintain that making and active imagination constitute the thread that joins all the peripheral tendencies within the modern tradition that resist the dualism of form and content, of signifier and signified.

The common factor of these peripheral tendencies is resistance to wholeness and externally imposed compositional order. Whereas Loos's aesthetics demands internal coherence, Adorno's suggests synthesizing the different interacting elements of the artistic imagination into an unhierarchical, porous field. For Adorno, it is exactly these "pores" and rifts that form the realm of artistic endeavor.

At the limit of these peripheral tendencies we find the idea of the art object as a self-creating, animated whole. This theory is presented, for example, by Heidegger, who sees art as something that to a certain degree has the capacity to create itself and its author.[12] Adorno and Bloch return to this idea from the point of view of Marxist criticism: they both believe that the making of art itself can become a realm that allows active intervention by a subject. In this process they consider ornament as a realm of real confrontation between human beings and the world; ornament becomes a site that invites us to go beyond the autonomous work of art, to see beyond form.

The criticism of Loos's status quo aesthetics can be summed up in Bloch's words: "the vital artistic element, which was the purpose of our quest, does not rest; it moves."[13] Ornament is understood as a dialectical image[14] in Benjamin's sense; it allows the superimposition of memory and a promise of transformation and evokes therefore a revolutionary meaning from within the work. Ornament becomes a necessary fragment[15] that breaks this continuity by destroying both art's appearance of totality and its temporal integrity. According to this interpretation it no longer refers to some reality beyond itself, but instead allows the subjective consciousness and reality to enter the art work.

Excess locates itself in the realm of materiality that constitutes the art work. Rather than settling into any fixed meaning, excess as ornament and ornament as excess introduce themselves as fields of action. The operative forces of ornamental motives such as symmetry, rotation, and repetition originate in the energy and transformation that lies within the productive system. The operative moves, which appear self-constitutive, thus question the subjective intentionality as such. This becomes clear when we look, for example, at Sullivan's ornaments and his design process: after a certain point the ornament takes over the geometric system that serves as a starting point. Adorno has this to say about excess: "The spirit of art is their plus or surplus—the fact that in the process of appearing they become more than they are."[16]

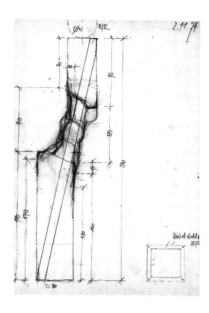

Right: Volker Giencke, column, 1974

Below: Louis Sullivan, *Fluent Parallelism* (Non-Euclidian), 1922

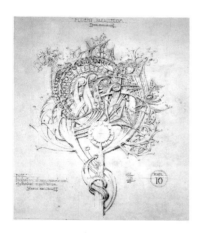

Ornament must therefore be understood as an architectural element that can cross over to this area where rules give way to free play, where subjective intentionality collides with what Agamben calls collective accumulation of experience, which finds its expression through repetition and rhythm. Ornament also reveals the impact issuing from the material and techniques available for the artist. It cannot be reduced to something designed solely from without; it gains its independence and power from within materiality as such.

Exceeding the figurative and linguistic levels of signification, ornament points out new directions to architecture; it represents certain capabilities embedded in the material and production itself. Understood in this way, it

Günther Domenig, Z-Bank, Vienna, 1979

Günther Domenig, Z-bank, interior

Günther Domenig, Steinhaus, Steindorf,
Carinthia, 1986–

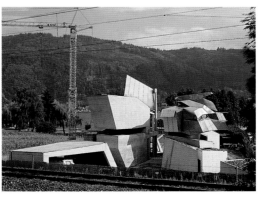

Volker Giencke, botanical garden, Graz,
1982–1995

Volker Giencke, botanical garden, general view of
the site

Volker Giencke, botanical garden, detail of the aluminum construction

Volker Giencke, Odörfer, showroom and warehouse, Klagenfurt, 1991 (photo: Paul Ott)

Volker Giencke, Odörfer, interior

Volker Giencke, Odörfer, glass roof with open
louvres

Helmut Richter, high school, Vienna, 1991–1994

Helmut Richter, high school, Vienna, interior of
the entrance hall

Volker Giencke, parish church, view of Aigen and
the bell tower (photo: Paul Ott)

Volker Giencke, parish church, Aigen, Ennstal,
1985–1992 (photo: Paul Ott)

Volker Giencke, Benedek House, Graz, 1986

Helmut Richter, Königseder House, Baum-
gartenberg, 1983

Klaus Kada, Tögl House, Graz, 1991

Helmut Richter, Brunnerstraße housing, view
facing the courtyard

Helmut Richter, Brunnerstraße housing, Vienna,
1991

Helmut Richter, Brunnerstraße housing, night
view

Klaus Kada, student housing, Graz, 1988–1992

Klaus Kada, student housing, close-up of
balconies

Volker Giencke, Maxonus boutique, Graz, 1986

Klaus Kada, Styrian glass-art center and glass
museum, Bärnbach, 1987–1988

Klaus Kada, glass museum, entrance

Wolfgang Feyferlik, Stockner House, Tainach,
Carinthia, 1991–1992

Volker Giencke, Spitzweggasse housing, Graz,
1987–1993

Volker Giencke, Kepler gymnasium, Graz,
1990–1992

Fredl Brambergerg, Tummelplatz, Graz, 1991
(photo: Paul Ott)

pulse gains ground when the real is called into question. Walter Benjamin's kinship with the surrealist tradition is based on his recognition of the productive and collective energy of the dream. Benjamin writes: "In the world's structure dream loosens individuality like a bad tooth. This loosening of the self by intoxication is, at the same time, precisely the fruitful, living experience that allowed these people to step outside the domain of intoxication."[18] Here, literally, the dream is understood as an individual healing process, as in the case of the fetish, which leads to the merging of the subjective and collective experience and consciousness.

In 1974 Henri Lefebvre introduced what he calls the psychoanalysis of space, which centers its argument exactly on all that Loos tried to eliminate from architectural discourse in the early twentieth century. Lefebvre seeks to reassess the correspondence among space, libidinal energy, and power. "Our space has strange effects. For one thing, it unleashes desire. It presents desire with 'transparency' which encourages it to surge forth in an attempt to lay claim to an apparently clear field."[19] He continues: "Any determinate and hence demarcated space necessarily embraces some things and excludes others; what it rejects may be relegated to nostalgia or it may be simply forbidden. Such a space asserts, negates and denies. It has some characteristics of a 'subject,' and some of an 'object.'"[20]

What the constitution of spatial psychoanalytics and the emphasis on materiality have in common is that they both try to break the illusion of the assumed neutrality of space. We can see that through the enhancement of materiality, structure, and detail, contemporary architecture departs from assumed neutrality based solely on formal and functional considerations in favor of ambience, and a particular ethos of the work. Such space eliminates the distance between subject and object, whereas neutral space keeps the distance necessary for disinterested, contemplative experience.

The idea of blurring the real and the imaginary through loss of objective distance returns in the postmodern discourse, which similarly questions the notions of authenticity and essence of art. Art becomes a play of signifiers lacking any fixed signifieds. Like the surrealist view of the psychopathological dream condition, postmodernism derives from subjective experience where various forms of mental distortion serve as a limit condition. Jameson's description of the space of a schizophrenic serves as a point of reference emphasizing materiality as an intensified sensuous experience: "The reduction of experience to 'pure and unrelated presents' further implies that the 'experience of the present becomes powerfully, overwhelmingly vivid and 'material': the world comes before the schizophrenic with heightened intensity, bearing the mysterious and oppressive charge of affect, glowing with hallucinatory energy.'"[21] In the fetish object, which for the surrealists is a model for a machine for desire, materiality and fragmentation trigger the intensification of experience through similar kinds of fragmentation and decontextualization. A particular moment of a detail is singled out as extraordinary; space turns into a virtual experience when the distance between subject and object has been lost.

The emphasis on structure and materiality in contemporary architecture can be evaluated against excess and the understanding of ornament as a trace of the human act. Through excess, architecture can unleash desire and prompt active imagination by losing the distance between subject and object. An intensified sense of materiality allows the transformation of the mere act of decoding or contemplation into a more active form of participation that can affect actual behavior; at its best, architecture so conceived triggers an intensified sense of being there, of belonging, that transcends the mere subjective experience. Following the existentialist idea of consciousness, a person comes to be understood through directionality toward the world, rather than as a self-contained monad.

When an architectural element such as ornament is singled out and turned into a material image, it enhances the sense of place, not only in the physical sense, but also by extending that vision to our imagination. This psychic realm of architecture understood as the correlation of place, image, and memory is familiar to us from the techniques of memorizing. The production of an image as a memory aid requires one to single out a detail and turn it into an extraordinary moment. Frances Yates quotes Cicero in *Ad Herennium*, who gives rules for the construction of such images that not only are able to enhance memory, but while so doing produce a kind of virtual reality that continues its existence in thought:

We ought, then, to set up images of a kind that can adhere longest in memory. And we shall do so if we establish similitudes as striking as possible; if we set up images that are not many or vague but active (imagines agentes); if we assign to them exceptional beauty or singular ugliness; if we ornament some of them, as with crowns or purple cloaks, so that the similitude may be more distinct to us; or if we somehow disfigure them, as by introducing one stained with blood or soiled with mud or smeared with red paint, so that its form is more striking, or by assigning certain comic effects to our images, for that, too, will ensure our remembering them more readily. The things we easily remember when they are real we likewise remember without difficulty when they are figments. But this will be essential—again and again to run over rapidly in the mind all the original places in order to refresh the images.[22]

Iain Richie, Reina Sofia Museum, Madrid, 1991,
glass elevator

This paragraph is a highly vivid description of Cicero's concept of image; essential is that an image is not only something solely visual, but includes a tangible, material presence; an image also is able to suspend the act. I therefore argue, based on Yates' discussion, that the material image has relevance to how we experience space by allowing an architectural experience to penetrate our imagination, our memory, by intensifying material presence and by suspending the act.

Close-ups

Detail and materiality gain importance when architecture loses fixed meaning. Like the fetish, a detail can step out of its context and constitute desire, which enables a new, engaged relationship with the world. Conceived as such, a detail can create new contextual readings around itself and has in this sense a function similar to that Deleuze ascribes to close-ups in film: "A close-up in film treats the face primarily as a face and the landscape; that is the definition of film, black hole and white wall, screen and camera. But the same goes for the earlier arts, architecture, painting, even the novel: close-ups animate and invent all of their correlations." [23]

What interests us here is how a detail relates to totality when it begins to have a life of its own. When this happens, it can blur or articulate differences between elements and materials, and it can choose either to intensify or nullify a sense of materiality. Similarly, it can either reveal or conceal the actual making process. The following examples show the shift toward an ambiguous yet intensified treatment of materials and details.

A comparison of Miesian glass architecture, its overarticulated detailing and its understanding of glass's materiality, with more contemporary examples of glass architecture shows how such blurring and lack of articulation correlate with another kind of sensitivity toward the material qualities of glass. Noteworthy is that Mies always frames glass between highly articulated mullions and thus freezes it into permanent inertia; glass is valued merely because it is transparent. In contemporary examples (I am referring to Giencke's Odörfer in Klagenfurt, Peter Rice's glass wall in the Cité de Science in Paris, Helmut Richter's Brunnerstraße housing complex in Vienna, and Ian Richie's extension to Reina Sofia Museum in Madrid), glass floats freely outside its carrying structure. The so-called Pilkington method invented by Rice is used by both Richter and Richie, whereas in Odörfer Giencke uses structural glazing in combination with the all-glass roof to allow a continuous glass surface. In comparison with two famous examples by Mies, the Barcelona pavilion and the National Gallery in Berlin, the continuous glass surface

Toward the Aesthetics

of the Incomplete

seems intensified and animated; the materiality of glass is celebrated by allowing its surface to fluctuate among the reflective, the opaque, and the transparent. *Blurring* and the lack of articulation of different elements allow the creation of a continuous surface and intensify the sense of materiality.

A similar type of blurring is apparent when we look at details of Benedek House and its surface created from glass and wood siding. The effect of suspension in the curved north facade blurs the materials into one tense surface that emphasizes thinness to gain intensity. Thus the house loses its form and becomes a continuous suspended surface in tension.

Looking at the entrance side of the facade, the details seem to contribute similarly not so much to the articulation of overall form, but rather to the creation of single images. The eye wanders from detail to detail, from the bamboo door handle to the louvered attic, from image to image. This intensification of fragments and shifting of focus result in a surface that radiates a sense of place defined by the intensification of pure material presence. Benedek House is a good example of a space and place that are defined by an intensified sense of details and materials, rather than being based on overall form and composition.

A feature that enhances materiality and similarly is able to sustain the act of making is *indexicality*. Indexicality means that a particular detail can simultaneously reveal and hide its actual making and articulation.

An example of the bravura of Giencke's highly personal sensibility toward detail can be found in the headquarters of the Styrian Association of Architects in downtown Graz. Here one sees how all mediating elements such as glass frames are eliminated in favor of a more surprising and confrontational collision of materials. Sudden penetrations are accentuated with color rather than hidden between surfaces. One finds interesting combinations and surprising collisions of structural elements. Old and new elements blur into unity without the customary overarticulation and didactic hierarchy often found in remodeling projects. Old elements are transformed and yield to new ones: a carrying wall is eliminated to open up a meeting area and is replaced by an iron beam accentuated with orange neon light. Only the inventiveness of such structural gymnastics bears a trace of the preexisting structure.

If we look at the close-ups of details in the collage prepared for publication, the approach to materials and details becomes clear: orientation, both with respect to location, as well as in terms of the horizontal and vertical hierarchy, is deliberately ambiguous. What we finally see are pictures without logic to tie them down to any single order and location; instead they join to form a landscape of materials and details. As in nature, whatever meaning

Helmut Richter, Brunnerstraße housing, Vienna,
1991, main elevation

Helmut Richter, Brunnerstraße housing, typical
apartment plan (ground floor)

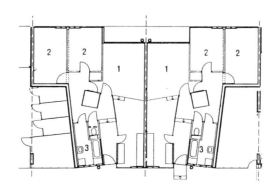

Toward the Aesthetics

of the Incomplete

Top: Volker Giencke, Benedek House, Graz, 1986,
view from the north

Bottom, left: Volker Giencke, Benedek House,
northeast corner

Bottom, right: Volker Giencke, Benedek House,
section drawing

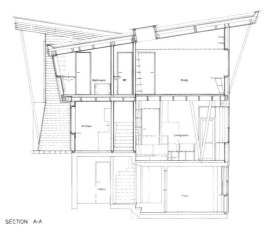

SECTION A-A

Volker Giencke, Benedek House, corner window
detail

there may be depends solely on the combination of such elements. Detail is essentially indexical: the tension between materials results from acts of penetration or elimination. This happens in purely material terms, without a literal translation of such acts into the expressive, formal elements that are typical of the projects by COOP Himmelblau.

A final technique for intensifying materiality exploits obscurity and *concealment*. Helmut Richter, unlike the more inconsistent and exuberant Giencke, is a good example. The difference in approach, becomes apparent at first glance, despite obvious similarities in their architectural language. In contrast to Giencke's blurring of colors and materials into a warm and gay ambience, Richter's projects appear more controlled and restrained. Giencke always attaches to hard materials such as glass, stainless steel, or aluminum a certain level of sensuousness and warmth by combining them with color or with wood. Richter's style relies almost exclusively on industrial materials and harsh primary colors. Emblematically, perhaps, Giencke prefers the ambiguous orange.

The sensuousness of Richter's projects is less noticeable. The apparent structural logic, which dominates the reading from outside, transforms into more fluid and less articulated spatial configurations when inside: Königseder House, Brunnerstraße housing, and the recent school building in Vienna demonstrate this strategy. The spatial fluidity is achieved by using slight angles both in section and in plan, which are barely noticeable, if at all, from outside. The dualism between exterior and interior reveals a certain sense of concealment familiar from Loos's houses as well as from rococo churches, where the austere exterior suddenly gives way to interior splendor and extravaganza.[24] Richter speaks of this Wittgensteinian metamorphosis from facts into something obscure into something whereof one cannot speak as follows: "Why decide not to put tiles in the [Seres] bathroom, which would most likely be much cheaper: the mirror makes the space appear much bigger, it gives it another light—but is this an argument? From here on there should be no more arguments because they would be ridiculous. Arguments pretend to be something which they cannot be by suggesting a logical relationship between things that don't exist, because the logical space is confined by language."[25] Richter follows Wittgenstein's dictum "ethics and aesthetics are one" exactly because of the obscure nature of both realms that exceeds mere rationality.

The most straightforward approach to detailing is Klaus Kada's. A contemporary of Giencke and Richter, Kada tends toward formal and structural articulation. His glass museum in Bärnbach near Graz is a good example: the

Top, left: Volker Giencke, remodeling of the headquarters of the Styrian Association of Architects and Engineers, Graz, 1983, details

Top, right: Volker Giencke, remodeling of the headquarters of the Styrian Association of Architects and Engineers, auditorium

Bottom: COOP Himmelblau, Atelier Baumann, Vienna, 1984

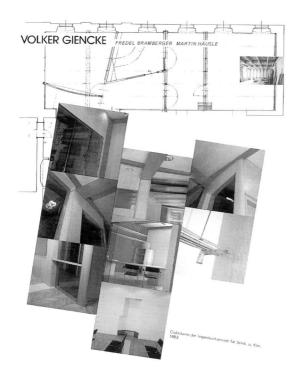

Toward the Aesthetics

of the Incomplete

Helmut Richter, Königseder House, Baumgarten-
berg, 1983, view from the street

Right: Helmut Richter, Königseder House, detail of the canopy and membrane

Middle: Helmut Richter, Königseder House, view from the garden

Bottom: Helmut Richter, Königseder House, ground floor plan

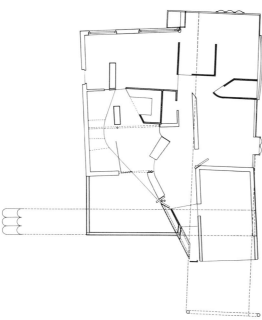

Adolf Loos, Möller House, Vienna, 1927–1928

Adolf Loos, Kärntner Bar, interior, Vienna, 1908

capacity of glass to blur distinctions is opposed to the clear formal segregation of different parts of the building. Kada's straightforwardness is perhaps at its best in his recent student housing project in Graz. The articulation of balconies with their red metal sheet railings turns into playful looseness.

These different approaches to detailing—blurring, indexicality, and obscuring—all serve the same purpose. What is at stake in all examples is the enhancement of materiality as such, devoid of the instrumentalization of function and structure or their taming by compositional form. This approach to materiality and detailing is apparent in Giencke's oeuvre: he seeks to intensify each material. For example, glass is truly glass, not merely something to be looked through when we see it as a suspended plane full of tension.

A project in which this material sensibility found a convincing realization is the boutique Maxonus, which also offers an intelligent solution to the restrictions imposed by the preexisting building, the postmodern opera extension on the corner of Kaiser-Josef-Platz in downtown Graz that dates from the early 1980s. The concrete slabs with their corrugated surface, which are meant as a kind of rustication and dominate the new opera extension, are turned into completely new architectural elements. The design encloses the corrugated slabs within the window display by putting a shallow glass box in front of the facade, a supplement similar to the strategies discussed with respect to the Red Stage that allows diversion in the pregiven condition. This move manifests Giencke's intention to destroy the pseudoclassical rustication of the preexisting opera extension. Especially at night the corrugated surface dissolves into magnificent rhythmic elements on which the light plays; the emphasis lies on the undulation of the concrete surface; structural elements have been turned into a single material image.

The project shows how the hermeneutic decoding of an element gives way to a reading based on materials and images; what prevails is the intensified sense of materiality freed of a fixed linguistic code. One can notice here a common tendency in contemporary Austrian architecture: any apparent code concerning the way materials are used is able to leap into the obscure and thus avoid easy categorization and reduction to any consistent material logic. Rather, one finds a tendency to strengthen the material image through fragmentation, intensification of tactility, and introduction of obstacles to the usual ways of decoding.

Enhancement of materiality, which escapes simple functional and structural signification, requires intensification on the level of details. According to Georges Didi-Huberman it is exactly the indexical detail that blurs the easy

Top, left: Andreas Stengg, Mariatrost Pilgrimage
Church, near Graz, 1714-

Top, right: Andreas Stengg, Mariatrost Pilgrimage
Church, interior

Bottom: Helmut Richter, Bad S. Seres, Vienna,
1983–1984

Klaus Kada, glass museum, Bärnbach, 1987–1988

Klaus Kada, glass museum, detail showing the entrance

Klaus Kada, student housing, Graz, 1988–1992

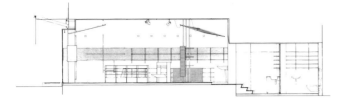

Left: Volker Giencke, Maxonus, longitudinal section

Middle: Volker Giencke, Maxonus boutique, Graz, 1986

Bottom: Volker Giencke, Maxonus, ground floor plan

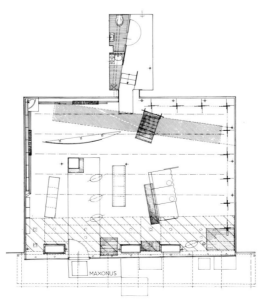

Volker Giencke, Maxonus, night view

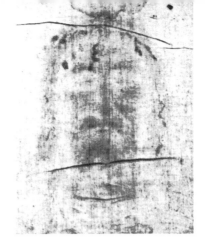

The Shroud of Turin

decoding of an image. He declares, "An intimate knowledge of this stained fabric is therefore an obstacle to discernment; because it gives priority to the materiality of the fabric, it compromises the hermeneutical process." [26] Didi-Huberman quotes Bachelard:

[Detail] is richness, but also uncertainty. Along with its subtle nuances occur profoundly irrational disturbances . . . At the level of detail, Thought and Reality appear to be set adrift from one another so that as Reality is distanced from the scale at which our thinking normally takes place, it loses its solidity in a certain way, its constancy, its substance. Finally, Reality and Thought are engulfed in the same nothingness. [27]

Didi-Huberman discusses the shroud of Turin in terms of visibility and nonvisibility, and how the desire to see leads us to the new locus of vision: that of phantasm. The other relevant point is how indexicality—the trace of a physical contact—by its very nature effaces figuration. Only due to this effacement is the original act sustained by the object. Indexicality, which in the shroud appears in the form of a stain, can be connected to the essential impurity present in crime and in ritual, always based on an act and followed by traces.

Detail finally leads to the matter of disfiguration and figuration due to its ability to constitute the relationship between whole and part, to decide between totality and fragmentation. A question is where to locate the ultimate moment of tension. As Adorno observes: "The authentic concept of tension emerges from that which is in a state of tension, namely form and its other, which is represented in the work by particularities." [28] He gives rank order to the movement toward incompleteness: "Art of the highest calibre pushes beyond totality towards a state of fragmentation." [29]

The discussion of materiality can therefore be tied to this question of form and its "other," where the other might be located in the act suspended in a fragment and leaving traces. Discernment of the hermeneutic process that Didi-Huberman talks about depends on a certain autonomy of single elements, where to retain a fixed conceptual level, the integrity of the work has to prevail. In both cases, materiality and detail relate to acts and temporality; even the authenticity of an art work, which Adorno refers to (hardly unaware of Heidegger's discussion) can be understood as a form of indexicality, as that which bears witness to "the leap," the ability of the work to create itself. The work is understood as a living thing with a certain symbolic thickness of meaning surrounding its presence.

Wolfgang Feyferlik, Stockner House, Tainach,
Carinthia, 1991–1992

Toward the Aesthetics

of the Incomplete

Machine Magic

Apart from the level of detail and material, structure also is able to mandate the shift toward the fictional. In this context, I will refer to structure as the realm wherein the transformation from the rational to the unknown and the impossible—even the magical—can take place.

This development can be considered a shift from the rational machine to the magical machine that is found when we look at postwar architecture in relation to technology. One sees a clear move away from the more aestheticizing tendencies of the so-called machine aesthetics of high modernism. Contemporary tendencies, apparent in high-tech, often manifest a more direct, even naive, relation with the machine. One must therefore distinguish between contemporary fascination with the machine and the formal, and the machine aesthetics found in purism and constructivism. The machine aesthetics of the first part of this century celebrated the machine as the ultimate emblem of the modern, expressing speed and other modernist sensibilities. For tendencies such as high-tech, the machine gains importance as an animated entity.

Again we see a trace of the surrealist heritage, which echoes a longer tradition within Western thought that is often forgotten. Surrealism's celebration of science and mathematics as something magical carries on a tradition based in medieval mysticism. In the Middle Ages the machine was celebrated for its occult power rather than for its logic and rationality. Good illustrations of this are Villard de Honnecourt's drawings of various machines that never reveal the secret of how they actually function. Similarly, surrealist objects were often depicted in the form of obscure machines.

A central concept of our discussion was introduced by Bacon: "There remains but mere experience, which when it offers itself is called change; when it is sought after, experiment." [30] Experimentation understood as a form of experience and imagination finally sets the limit to the subject's control of his or her own endeavor. The ultimate expression for the tension between individual creativity and available tools is found in experimentation; pushing the available technical means has an element of change and surprise that the surrealists emphasized in their work. So conceived, structure finally surpasses art and architecture as an expression of subjective creativity and intentionality. Adorno describes experimentation as follows: ". . . experimental work must contain qualities that were unforeseeable in its process of production; or, to put it in subjective terms, the artist has to be surprised by what he creates." [31] It takes place when intuition finds ultimate expression in its relationship to the tools and techniques available.

Top, left: Villard de Honnecourt, machines, 1225–1250

Middle: Hans Bellmer, *The Machine Gunneress in a State of Grace,* 1937

Bottom: Jean Tinguely making the relief *Éloge de la Folie* in his studio, Soisy-sur-Ecole, 1966

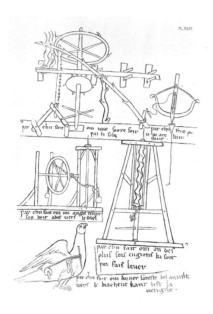

Toward the Aesthetics

of the Incomplete

The concept of experimental architecture has to be extended beyond the trivial understanding of experimenting as an endless breaking of rules and challenging of existing norms. It is against this background that we have to understand the current emphasis of experimentation in contemporary Austrian architecture. Adorno's discussion is a point of reference:

There was in this notion a latently traditionalistic presupposition that tolerated experimentation provided its results were going to be tested against the established norms, perhaps legitimating the former, perhaps not. This conception of what artistic experimentation is is widely—and wrongly—accepted even today. Today the underlying faith in continuity and therefore the concept of experimentation itself have become problematic. While experimentation has survived as a synonym for certain methods in art, it has come to designate something completely different, namely that the artistic subject uses methods the results of which it cannot foresee. This change, which coincided roughly with the shift of aesthetic interest away from expressive subjectivity over to objective consistency, is not altogether unheard-of. The idea of construction, which has been fundamental to modernism, has always implied the primacy of constructive methods over subjective imagination. Construction necessitates solutions that are not immediately present or obvious to the senses. The unforeseen, then, not only is a contingent effect but also has a moment of objectivity, today more so than ever. Disenfranchised by an independently evolving technology, the subject raises its disenfranchisement to the level of consciousness, one might almost say to the level of a programme for artistic production. Failing that, the subject at least manifests an unconscious desire to blunt the impact of impending heteronomy by making it a moment of the productive process alongside the subjective starting-point. This process is facilitated by the fact that imagination, which is the passage of the work through the subject, is not some fixed quantity but a variable, as Heinz Stockhausen rightly pointed out. Imagination can be blunt or keen. Now, modernism has contributed a specific technique to art, which is to have a blunt imagination of something and underscore precisely the vagueness of that imagination—a veritable balancing of the experimenting artist.[32]

In this context I challenge Frampton's understanding of technology as a universalizing and homogenizing force that is contrasted by regional crafts and materials. In Austrian architecture experimentation is understood as something that has the ability to transform existing technologies by challenging the limits of technology in particular and the human being's will for control in general. Unlike Frampton, I am not willing to see the organic and the mechanic principles as two opposing poles of the modern tradition, but consider them to coexist in a continuous dialogue. The ambiguity so created is not so different from the surrealist blurring of inanimate and animate; architecture occupies the zone in between.

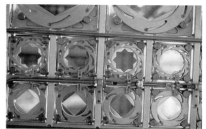

The new attitudes toward structure as a realm for experimentation are manifest in Giencke's glasshouses in the botanical garden. The structure is exaggerated to the point of obsessive repetition of the same element: the hollow parabolic arch. Tiltedness, which serves a functional purpose by creating various heights of space for plants of various heights, emphasizes the structure's unsettled character. The effect of zooming space thus created, which becomes shallower or more extended, depending on the point of perception, shows how the construction of static reality crosses over into the realm of the impossible, from the logical into the magical realm.[33] (To allow a figurative moment to occur, the fact that the structure is conceived as a giant radiator supports the impression that architecture not only imitates the machine aesthetically, but actually turns into a machine of sorts itself.)

When experimentation exceeds mere problem solving, it reaches toward a higher form of imagination that exceeds mere rationality, becoming what the surrealist would call superrationality, or that which by pushing the rational into extreme makes it reveal its origin in the obscure and the magical. Experimentation was founded as a realm where rationality enters creativity and the other way around; a perfect liminality where these two poles constantly correct and comment on each other without one taking over. Experimentation becomes the ultimate expression of sublation, which has the capacity of simultaneous negation and affirmation. Opposed to the negative avant-garde techniques of Dada and expressionism, where expressive freedom and unreality end up confirming rationality, experimentation employs a more subtle technique of blurring the difference between unreality and reality. Such blurring characterizes the approach in Giencke's botanical garden project as well as in Richter's subtle inversions of structural articulation and ambiguous spatial strategies. Both Giencke's and Richter's works tend to push logic toward the accidental. They recall the Wittgensteinian paradigm between language (architecture) and things. Architecture belongs, for the likes of Giencke and Richter, to the latter category, drawing from the tension of logical reasoning and the realm beyond: "In the world everything is as it is and happens as it does happen."[34]

The development away from machine aesthetics toward what I call machine mysticism, which can be characterized as fascination with the machine as an animated entity, demands closer scrutiny. This reappropriation of machine aesthetics and its relationship to new technologies is relatively recent. I will sketch here some notions about the relationship between architecture and technology that are relevant to our discussion.

Volker Giencke, botanical garden, (*a*) detail of the acrylic glazing, and (*b*) detail of the cast aluminum joint

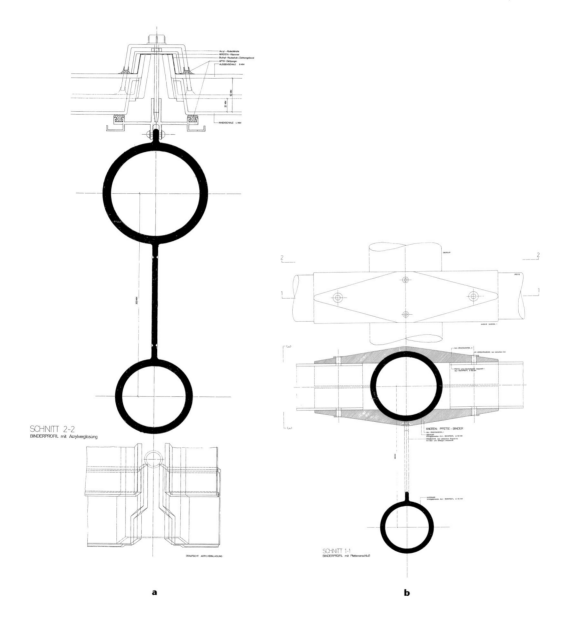

SCHNITT 2-2
BINDERPROFIL mit Acrylverglasung

SCHNITT 1-1
BINDERPROFIL mit Plattenanschluß

a

b

Two major steps are taken in the postwar period: in the late 1950s the architectural avant-garde experiments with prefabrication using models from the automobile and airplane industries; the engineer-architect Jean Prouvè is a major innovator in this area. The second move happens in late 1960s as architecture moves toward the fantastic. The projects of the London-based Archigram group borrow from science fiction. The limit condition produced by both moves is the paradigm of the building as a kind of equipment. Architecture finally becomes totally responsive to human action and movement, even animated.

The auto industry lends itself as a model not only in terms of production but also in terms of mobility and the nonpermanency of taste and design. The models taken from both mass culture and mass production support the ideology of temporality, flexibility, and nonmonumental architecture, where the user chooses, readapts, and finally has the freedom to neglect the object when it ceases to fulfill its "equipmentality." The problem posed by instrumentalization is that it causes the will for mastery, as Heidegger concluded: through mastery, technology's true magic to create something that exceeds the known and the commonplace escapes our notice.[35]

In the German-speaking realm, perhaps the most influential innovator in the postwar period was Frei Otto, who is credited for introducing a certain poetics into structural thinking and a fresh understanding of technology's potentials. The tentlike structures built for the 1972 Olympic games in Munich in collaboration with Günther Behnisch may be the most fantastic example of the blurring of landscape and architecture. Here architecture creates an artificial, illusionary landscape, and anyone who has visited the site, especially at sunset, will share my opinion. Otto developed the idea of tensile structure and set new standards for using technology; architecture was not to mimic the machine, but found its own way of dealing with the possibilities created by new materials and technologies, possibilities that, for example, in the case of these tensile structures, correlated with old building traditions, such as nomad tents. Conceived as contemporary rather than as anachronistic construction, they illustrate what Benjamin calls "the echo of the archaic within the new."[36]

Perhaps the most influential tendency, one that sums up the development from the late 1950s onward, is metabolism, initiated by a Japanese group of architects formed by Kiyonori Kikutake, Kisho Kurokawa, Fumihiko Maki, and Masato Otaka. Their manifesto "Metabolism 1960—A Proposal for New Urbanism," dating from 1958, proclaims the following: "We regard human society as a vital process, a continuous development from atom to

Top left: Jean Prouvé, own house, Nancy, 1953

Cedric Price, Fun Palace, project, 1961

Renzo Piano and Richard Rogers, Centre Beaubourg, Paris, 1975, rear elevation

Bottom: Renzo Piano and Richard Rogers, Centre Beaubourg, casting of gerberettes

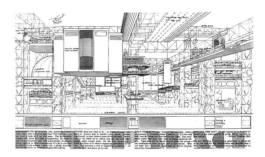

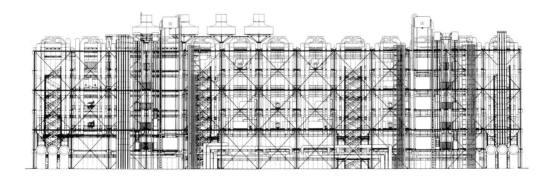

Günther Behnisch together with Frei Otto, Olympic stadium, Munich, 1967–1972, detail of the roof construction

nebula. The reason why we use the biological word *metabolism* is that we believe that metabolism indicates only acceptance of a natural, historical process, but we are trying to encourage the active metabolic development of our society through our proposals."[37]

The key premises for this statement were, first, that human society must be regarded as one part of a continuous natural entity, and, second, that technology is an extension of humanity. Whereas Western society still was trying to solve the conflict between humanity and science, the metabolists believed technology to be in tune with Buddhist tradition and nature, and that therefore technology and humanity belong together. For them, architectural space was a space in between rather than based on enclosure and fixed form. It was characterized by the fluidity and transformations that take place in time; the aesthetics of metabolism came to be defined as "aesthetics of time."[38] Metabolist aesthetics, and the metabolists themselves, were based on the Buddhist concept of *ma*, a "moment of immobility when change is indicated" (Kurokawa).[39]

The most important things introduced by the metabolists into the international architectural discourse are, on one hand, temporality and transformability, and on the other, integration of the mythical into technology. The metabolists understood structure as flexibility and endless transformation; in fact, the etymological root of the word metabolism means transformation and changeability. Structure has taken either forms of nature or the mythic forms of architectural history.

On a conceptual level the metabolists are the first to discover the liminal condition of spatial thinking in traditional Japanese architecture. The *en*-space—in-between space—that they rediscovered and thematized emphasizes the temporal aspect of architecture as opposed to Western permanence and monumentality. This spatial liminality, already present in the traditional Japanese house, is relevant for the European development of a new sensitivity toward boundaries and new concepts in spatial thinking that exceed that of formal enclosure, based on the duality between inside and outside. Japanese architectural thinking was influential in both practice and theory; a similar sensitivity toward space and place starts to emerge both in the texts of phenomenological theoreticians and in built projects.

A desire to push architecture toward undecidability and liminality, in directions that evoke this Japanese idea of *en*-space, can be found in techniques that emphasize ephemerality. This means a return to one of the most common formal tropes of twentieth-century architecture: the floating house. The best example is Mies van der Rohe's Farnsforth House. This paradigmatic

Toward the Aesthetics

of the Incomplete

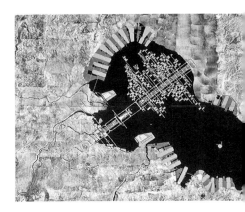

Kenzo Tange, Tokyo Bay project, 1960 (photo: Kawasumi)

move repeats itself in the obsession of many contemporary projects with elimination of the wall and rejection of the limitations of gravity.

In many projects—Giencke's Odörfer, the Aigen church, Benedek House, and the Spitzweg housing project; Richter's Königseder House and his recent school project—one finds exaggeration of the roof and partial or total elimination of the wall as a clearly articulated element. The horizontal, or semihorizontal, roof structures are elaborated and favored in relation to the vertical, supportive elements. The latter are minimalized and made to disappear. The roof as a floating, trembling element illustrates architecture as suspended between earth and sky, instead of occupying space. The roof becomes the most suggestive and magical of all elements. Unlike the wall, it creates space without enclosure. This recalls Konrad Wachsmann's space-grid roof structures that extend infinitely. The minimalized impact on the earth's surface in Giencke's single-family houses also supports the idea of floating, which reveals the attitude behind this gesture. Ephemerality is given priority over eternity in a way that recalls the Japanese sensibility.

The metabolist ideology characterized by this Eastern sensitivity influenced European architectural discourse since the 1960s in many different ways; the floating architecture paradigm is only one example of how sensitivity to space and structure changed and helped to reassess the vocabulary of modern architecture. There are also more literal and direct influences, both formal and ideological. First is the formal translation of metabolist language found in mega-structures and high-tech. Metabolism takes architectural form to be related to biological forms, allowing growth and transformation. In Graz its influence is most evident in the Ragnitz project by Günther Domenig and Eilfried Huth. It also is manifest in several other conceptual projects all over Austria. The other influence has more to do with the religiomythic sensitivity of the East.

A trace of the metabolist ideology of integrating mythical forms with those related to the machine is found in what can be characterized as organic high-tech; the extravaganza of Domenig's Z-Bank, and the approach taken by COOP Himmelblau are examples. Similar tendencies still prevail in Japanese architecture: Takasaki Masaharu, a former collaborator of Domenig, and Team Zoo are perhaps the most extreme examples. Apart from Domenig and COOP Himmelblau, one finds subtle examples of organic high-tech in the work at the Architectural Association, especially in the mid-1980s; Chris McDonald and Peter Salter are the first ones who come to mind. Characteristically, these tendencies take technology to the realm of mythic; structural load-bearing systems are difficult to trace, hierarchies are blurred, horizontal and

Kisho Kurokawa, helix structure, 1961

Kisho Kurokawa, agriculture city plan, 1961

vertical order are destroyed. Organic form begins to emerge and, as in the Z-Bank, buildings take on an uncanny, animated character. Common to all these examples is that architectural form finally reaches animation, which becomes its absolute challenge and limit. Architecture is understood as perpetually incomplete, and therefore it opens itself to chance and change in ways that echo surrealist sensibilities.

Machine mysticism opens structural thinking to what lies beyond functional considerations. Within structure it exceeds the formalistic understanding of metabolist techniques that turn structure into a diagram. To do justice to the metabolist legacy, the understanding of structure as a mere system must be rejected in favor of conceiving it as an event. That is, rather than settling for a fixed system, structure opens possibilities for transformation, enhancing an ambience of undecidability, liminality, and being in between. Opposed to the machine aesthetic of earlier periods, more contemporary machine mysticism can be characterized by its negation of any fixed system as an architectural paradigm. Common to all these strategies is the will to avoid unity and completeness. The celebration of materiality and structure manifests the will to resist the hegemony of compositional, abstract order.

Once more we have to return to indexicality and act. But we also should explore the way architecture presents itself not so much as a self-referential entity, but as something that is about a certain attitude. The metabolist heritage becomes apparent in the coexistence of technology and imagination in contemporary architecture, which, like en-space, opens itself as a realm of possibilities rather than solutions and facts.

The fascination with technology must be understood in this context of potentiality, as material for imagination to go beyond mere factuality. Metabolism echoes Benjamin's idea that technological wish images always derive from the mythic past. In Benjaminian terms, "technology's capacity to create the not-yet-known" mediates between past and present, forming a wishimage, which depends on the transformation and mediation of matter relevant to utopian consciousness.[40] Susan Buck-Morss elaborates on Benjamin's understanding of the relationship between technology and imagination as follows.

It could be said that for Benjamin progressive cultural practice entails bringing both technology and imagination out of their mythic dream states, through making conscious the collective's desire for social utopia, and the potential of the new nature to achieve it by translating that desire into the "new language" of its material forms. Benjamin writes that in the nineteenth century, the development of the technical forces of production "emancipated the creative forms (Gestaltungsformen) from

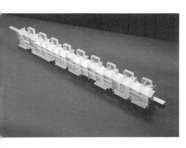

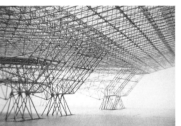

*art, just as in the sixteenth century the sciences liberated themselves from philosophy." This is quite
an extraordinary claim. It implies that, just as reason ("the sciences"), once having become secular-
ized ("liberated from philosophy"), became free to be applied instrumentally to processes of social
production, so imagination, inspired by "the creative forms" of technology and diverted from purely
aesthetic goals (that is, "emancipated form art"), can be applied to the task of constructing a new
basis for collective social life.*[41]

Following Benjamin's wish-image, one can understand the difference
between two approaches to materiality and structure. One insists on the act
of creation, and the other projects itself toward the future. It is the latter approach that interests us here: the material manifestation of technology understood as a Blochian anticipatory illumination of the not-yet rather than the
no-more of the creation process. Technology today is needed not so much to
celebrate its modern appeal or the genius of *Homo faber*, but rather to allow
architecture to project itself into the future as an embodiment of a promise
for a better world. To do that, architecture has to exceed all merely formal and
aesthetic considerations and extend itself toward the ethical and communal.
Technology serves this purpose well. Due to the accumulation of modern
experience based on innovation, technology has gained the allegorical and
poetic depth necessary for it to be something that combines the "practical,
symbolic and the imaginary"[42] levels and therefore possesses the capacity for
gesturing toward a utopian community. It is exactly this gesture that should
interest us.

The Veil: Architecture without Organs

Didi-Huberman's view of detail collides with the aim of a good part of
the twentieth-century avant-garde: the elimination of representation, of
mimesis, of the duality between signifier and signified, of form and content.
When evaluating this shift, the question becomes whether or not the move
away from hermeneutic reading to hermetic text is, as Renato Poggioli suggests, a social task.

The new sensibility toward materiality and structure, which has been
set free from functional ordering principles, liberates architecture from its
traditional modes of representation based on the interdependence of form
and content. Architecture comes rather to be defined as a physical object
characterized by the transmission of a certain character and ambience, as a
physical condition marked by a human act and attitude.[43] We can call such
a physical demonstration a gesture. We can therefore continue to ask how
architecture is able to sustain this attitude, this gesture, as a fetish is able to
sustain a memory of an act.

Right: Günther Domenig and Eilfried Huth,
Ragnitz project, Graz, 1967

Top, left: Wilhelm Holzbauer, helicopter high-rise,
1962

Top, right: Marete Mattern in collaboration with
Volker Giencke, town planning for Ratingen,
1972

Bottom: Chris McDonald and Peter Salter, ICI
trade pavillion, competition entry, 1983

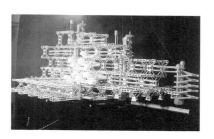

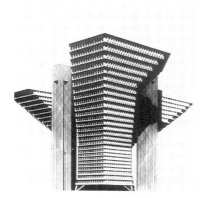

Toward the Aesthetics

of the Incomplete

Gesture refers to movements and attitudes of the body, not the functioning of the body. A gesture can be understood as an "outward physical expression of the inward soul."[44] Agamben writes, "What characterizes gesture is that in it there is neither production nor enactment, but undertaking and supporting. In other words, gesture opens the sphere of *ethos* or the most fitting sphere of the human."[45]

Therefore, to understand how architecture can make a statement, as the avant-garde has tried to do, we have to reassess the analogy between body and architecture in the light of gesture. Just as we imagine the body being a transmitter of what lies within, architecture can function as a transmitter of the ethical in its thinking. Central is that a gesture is an act, a movement that is not motivated by the body's needs or its functioning, but by its desires and attitudes. The traditional understanding of the body as the abode of the soul has to be reassessed; consciousness, or soul if you wish, is rather to be understood as "consciousness of something," as Sartre observed, always directed out toward something, without having a content in itself.

To clarify this analogy between body and architecture, I quote Bachelard:

The phenomenology of the poetic imagination allows us to explore the being of man considered as the being of a surface, of the surface that separates the region of the same from the region of the other. It should not be forgotten that in this zone of sensitized surface, before being, one must speak, if not to others, at least to oneself. . . . It would be contrary to the nature of my inquiries to summarize them by means of radical formulas, by defining the being of man, for example, as the being of an ambiguity. I only know how to work with a philosophy of detail. Then, on the surface of being, in that region where being wants to be both visible and hidden, the movements of opening and closing are so numerous, so frequently inverted, and so charged with hesitation, that we could conclude on the following formula: man is a half-open thing.[46]

Pursuing the analogy of body and architecture through gesture and ambiguity, we arrive at the envelope itself, the surface of the boundary as the most decisive architectural element. The boundary is where different intensities, including attitudes, unfold, and therefore is the most ambiguous element of all, the one that has the capacity to reveal and to conceal. It belongs to neither the interior nor the exterior and has, by its very nature, the power to question this preliminary segregation in architecture: inside versus outside, form versus content, body versus soul. The boundary is therefore the political architectural element per se.

Gianlorenzo Bernini, *The Ecstacy of Saint Theresa,*
Rome, 1645–1652

Michelangelo, *Atlas (Il Prigione),* Florence, ca.
1519

The boundary finally decides what becomes visible and what stays concealed. Lefebvre writes: "Consider the great power of a façade, for example. A façade admits certain acts to the realm of what is visible, whether they occur on the façade itself (on balconies, window ledges, etc.) or are to be seen from the façade (processions in the street, for example). Many other acts, by contrast, it condemns to obscenity: these occur *behind* the façade. All of which already seems to suggest a 'psychoanalysis of space.'"[47] Here we should keep in mind Loos's architecture, in which façade simply segregates and conceals, and therefore insists on the segregation of private and public, as well as on social integrity and status quo. What is at stake in the contemporary view of façade is that it always carries a promise of revelation and of breaking boundaries.

What Lefebvre calls the "psychoanalysis of space" and the politics of concealing versus revealing finally leads to questions about the erotics of architecture. "In the figurative arts, eroticism appears as a relationship between clothing and nudity. Therefore, it is conditional on the possibility of movement—transit—from one state to the other,"[48] writes Mario Perniola and, ". . . transit does exist between the visible and the invisible, between clothing and what it covers."[49]

In this context, transit becomes a condition that is emblematic of the whole avant-garde tradition; a transit between the promise and its delivery, between the idea and its realization, between the real and the unreal, between individual and community. Curiously literal translations of this understanding of the transit zone are made when the boundary begins to show signs of animation.

Traces of Austria's baroque heritage are preserved in contemporary sensibilities of the boundary. Perniola discusses the baroque view of what he calls the erotic transit as follows: "The transit [movement] established between clothing and nudity shows up in two fundamental ways: in the use of the erotics of drapery or attire, as we see in Bernini, and in the depiction of the body as a living garment, as we see in anatomical illustrations." [50] Two kinds of elements are at stake: the veil and the skin.

Perniola elaborates on erotic transit:

It is necessary to keep these premises in mind in order to fully understand the extraordinary erotic magic of Bernini's masterpiece, the Ecstasy of Saint Theresa, made for the Cornaro chapel in the Church of Santa Maria della Vittoria in Rome. Its magic does not depend simply upon the angel's splendor, the evident sexual symbolism of the arrow, or upon the expression that crosses the saint's lovely face, clearly indicating that she is about to faint, but mostly on the fact that Saint Theresa's body disappears in the drapery of her tunic. It has undergone a transformation that has emancipated it from human form, while it still projects all the impetuous and vibrant shuddering of a body in ecstasy. . . . By conceding less to the formal unity of the work, it accentuates the essential: the transit between body and clothes, the displacement of what lies beneath the drapery. . . . The sacramental presence is a living presence; it is "an ever renewed motion . . . that sees clearly how form is only one aspect of what exists." It does not find peace, rest or repose in a pleasing surface, nor in a spiritual marriage nor in theatricality as an end in itself. Rather, it tirelessly and continually flows, ebbs, moves and shifts. [51]

When discussing the contemporary concepts of enclosure and boundary one can find architectural translations of both of them introduced by Perniola: the skin and the veil. They require two structural approaches as well as two strategies. The skin implies a boundary suspended between inside and outside; it requires a certain tension. The veil on the other hand implies wrapping that can be removed. It suggests secrecy yet promises revelation.

Let us look at examples. As discussed in previous chapters, the botanical garden is an ultimate example of the skin. Whereas the body conceived as a half-open thing negates the notion of an enclosed or unified entity, the skin must form an adaptable and elastic surface. The acrylic skin in the botanical

Top: Volker Giencke, botanical garden, end of subtropic house

Middle: Volker Giencke, Helsinki Museum of Contemporary Art, competition entry, 1992, elevation drawing

Bottom: Volker Giencke, Helsinki Museum of Contemporary Art, model

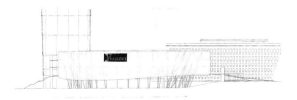

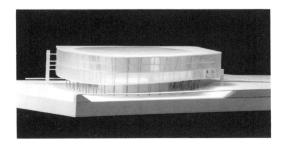

Toward the Aesthetics

of the Incomplete

Opposite, left to right: Volker Giencke, project for a
carpentry school, Murau, 1988

Volker Giencke, law school at the University of
Graz, competition entry, Graz, 1985

Volker Giencke, roofing of Helsinki railway
station, competition project, 1994

Middle: Volker Giencke, Helsinki railway station,
the roof

Bottom: Volker Giencke, Odörfer, the veil

garden reflects this view of an adaptable surface. It appears as if in tension and it adapts to the conditions of breathing, the requirements of ventilation and exit, in a flexible manner. We might as well accept a slip into the figurative reading. The building reminds us of dinosaurs. Conceived as a skin, the boundary becomes a kind of "osmotic membrane" (Virilio): a zone between two atmospheres, between two intensities.[52]

Whereas the skin marks a difference, the veil always implies covering something. Concealment and disappearance of a veiled object can mean two things: "plus value of loss, of absence," as proposed by Dominique Laporte in discussing Christo's wrappings,[53] or what Derrida calls the "subsidy/bonus of seduction," that is, seduction understood as a supplement.[54] The former implies obtrusiveness, where what is covered gains its true nature only by being absent. The latter, on the other hand, means that the act of concealment, the tease, is itself a productive act that triggers desire. The veil has to have a life of its own, it has to fluctuate and tremble, and most of all, it has to promise the act of unveiling.

In Odörfer the veil recalls the sensuality of something wrapped around the body. The act of wrapping is exaggerated by separating the glazing from the carrying construction; hangers made of bent wire convey the image of a cloth or a curtain hung from the structure: something extra. During construction the "something put in front" became a culmination point: the glass made the expressive and dynamic steel structure appear more subtle and ambiguous and lose its functional meaning. The glass surface added a new dimension (supplement) to the structure by the simultaneous act of veiling the functional and unveiling the ambiguous material image.

The structure—the naked truth—is made ambiguous through veiling. The veil prevents the architecture from turning into an ontological stasis, from reaching the limit that is found in structure, which can be said to represent only itself through ordering. The glass surface wrapped around the construction itself represents this limit condition: the veil, as Perniola writes "is not a mere obstacle to seeing with a naked eye, but actually the condition that makes vision possible."[55] Unlike the modernist conception of glass architecture, the act of disappearance is the reverse. Normally, an opaque surface is visible and transparency is invisible, but the glass roof of Odörfer challenges our habitual ways of seeing: the transparent (uncovered) state makes possible the presence of the ultimate architectural, the structure, by revealing its own limit condition.

The new glass architecture is generally more about this ability to avoid stasis by suspending the moment prior to unveiling than it is about transpar-

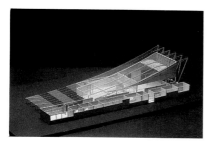
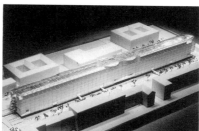
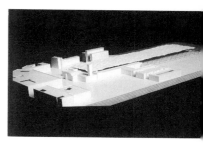

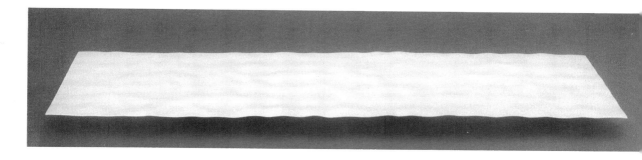

ency and revelation. Tied to the economics of desire, like the body that is both veil and veiled, it becomes a transit zone that cannot be possessed, but signifies a way to architecture, its rediscovery. Therefore glass can hardly be reduced to continuity or clarity, but should be considered as veiling, the most ambiguous gesture that modern architecture has yet produced: the erotic transit that promises the possibility of movement from one state to another. Transit, or Heideggerian unfolding, is based on the tension between the veil and that which it covers, between the visible and the invisible. Perceived as such, architecture is able to fuse and condense meaning rather than separate and clarify it, and thus evoke the symbolic and poetic within the modern tradition.

Toward the Aesthetics

of the Incomplete

Gestern war der zerstörende Avant-Gardist, morgen wird es der
bejahende, wird es der Liebende sein.[1]

—**Monsignore Otto Mauer**

Architecture must advance by taking emotionally moving situations, rather than emotionally moving forms, as the material it
works with. And the experiments conducted with this material
will lead to unknown forms.[2]

—**Guy Debord**

Reconstructing Experience

When evaluating contemporary Austrian architecture it is important to
trace the particular artistic and intellectual climate in which the reassessment of the modern tradition
occurred. At this point one can sum up the main techniques: the challenging
of spatial closure and static form; negation of traditional modes of representation; technological and material experimentation; integration of nature and
lived experience; and celebration of immediacy in the design process.

A common denominator of the techniques is the will to invest architecture with the emancipatory potential of the avant-garde and the mythical potential within the modern tradition. What is proposed is a strategy for *engaged*
architecture. The emphasis on temporality opposed to the stasis of spatial closure aims to go beyond the mere objecthood and the visual. Peripheral notions discussed in this book evoke the fictional within the modern tradition
and are the key to understanding how contemporary ideas of engagement
relate to the twentieth-century architectural tradition.

The will to belong to the avant-garde community is supported by the
fact that the architectural discourse from the late 1960s on shared the premises of its project, including vigorous attempts by artists and architects to
organize themselves into groups to form programs for engaged art and architecture. The use of avant-garde rhetoric is a common feature in catalytic
groups such as COOP Himmelblau, Haus-Rucker-Co, Salz der Erde, Zünd up,
and Missing Link in the realm of architecture, and Wiener Aktionisten in the
realm of art.

The Red Stage is emblematic of the new avant-garde: while challenging
the strategies of the historical avant-garde, the new tendencies share the pathos and goals of previous avant-gardes that follow Breton's famous formula:
"Marx said, 'Change the world,' Rimbaud said, 'Change life.'" On the whole,
the architectural community still seems to have a strong belief in the social
relevance of architecture. In this chapter I will discuss how contemporary
architectural discourse in Austria relates to the postwar debate on the validity
of the avant-garde project, and the role of art and architecture in the society.

Haus-Rucker-Co, Balloon for Two, Vienna, 1967

Art's special place in society in countries such as Austria, which faced a crisis after the war, was based on its ability to create new material realities, rather than merely to depict existing ones. The individual caught up in an ideological and textual web finds the way out through an imaginary experience triggered by material events, which orients social reality toward the future.

The role of the avant-garde has always been to search for freedom within a given system. Two notions anticipate that freedom: desire and the abyss of nothingness. If the earlier avant-garde led to the latter state—Malevitch's *Black Square* may be its most emblematic art work—the postwar Austrian avant-garde believed that engaged art can find its answer within the former. The strategy of desire cannot be based on the binary opposition of meaning and rationality; it has to believe in the extension of what is commonly understood as meaning. This is where structure and materiality become important for engaged architecture. The experience of sensuous materiality differs from the cathartic strategies of the earlier pictorial avant-gardes. Able to open up a space for imaginative freedom, the sensuous, rather than the pictorial, can carry meaning that reaches beyond the contemplative experience that leads to the abyss of nothingness.

Defining the relationship to the avant-garde tradition becomes the main issue Austrian art discourse since the late 1950s. Socially engaged art gets a new interpretation that shuns direct ideological and social criticism. Whereas the established definition of the avant-garde assumes it can exist only in a critical and nonaffirmative sense, the Austrian redefinition reflects another kind of tendency: the possibility of experience became the main issue. Robert Fleck describes the position as follows: "The goal of this avant-garde was to expand the subjective (the inner world), to interpret its own activities by means of the concept of 'post-object-art' (art of ideas, of individuation), fluctuating between melancholy and sadness."[3]

The leading figure in the discourse was Monsignore Otto Mauer, priest, spiritual leader, public figure, and art critic. He was the founder and long-time curator of the *Galerie nächst St. Stephan,* which became one of the most important Austrian art institutions in the era after the war. Characteristic of Mauer's role was his function as a bridge among cultural life, the Catholic Church, and politics. In his role as curator, Mauer started to define the position and means of modern, especially avant-garde, art through his selection of artists to exhibit, his organization of lectures, and the many essays and speeches he delivered between circa 1950 and the 1970s. He promoted symbiosis between modern art and the Catholic Church by emphasizing their common ethical and moral functions. Hans Sedlmayr was Mauer's opponent in the *Streit um die moderne Kunst* (struggle for modern art), which was triggered by Sedlmayr's *Verlust der Mitte* (*The Lost Center*; *Art in Crisis*), published in 1948. Whereas Sedlmayr thought modern art was anti-Christian, Mauer believed that it could share the same *Weltanschauung* as the Church.

Mauer's position was exactly the opposite of pessimistic critical theory, asserting that both art and Church can reappropriate the concept of freedom for society. When explaining the concept of freedom, he emphasizes the following: "The church has therefore an emancipatory character; yet it doesn't remain struck with the negative 'freedom from,' but turns towards the 'freedom for' the great creative tasks of mankind." [4] The Austrian avant-garde sets itself apart from ideological criticism and focuses on the ethical and moral functions of art.

The organization of experience becomes the main issue in the redefinition of socially engaged art after the Second World War. Art should reflect the human condition rather than the ideological and institutional structures in which the subject and the object exist. To trigger and simultaneously organize such experience, art is to produce material experiences—to some extent, reproduce the real—rather than represent any outside reality. In doing this the avant-garde sets itself against representation and mimesis. This *Hunger nach den Realen* (hunger for the real) supports the same duality of life and representation that we find in Derrida's appraisal of Artaud:

The theater of cruelty is not a representation. It is life itself, in the extent to which life is unrepresentable. Life is the nonrepresentable origin of representation. "I have therefore said 'cruelty' as I might have said 'life'." This life carries man along with it, but is not primarily the life of man. The latter is only a representation of life, and such is the limit—the humanist limit—of the metaphysics of classical theater." The theater as we practice it can therefore be reproached with a terrible lack of imagination. The theater must make itself the equal of life—not an individual life, that individual aspect of life in which CHARACTERS triumph, but the sort of liberated life, which weeps away human individuality and in which man is only a reflection. [5]

This redefinition of the avant-garde emphasizes its ultimate goal: to unite art with life. To test the goal's validity, the avant-garde project in general and postwar art and architecture in particular had to move beyond the cultural pessimism characteristic of poststructuralist thought. If language is already corrupted, another kind of life, outside or within language, is yet to be discovered. The avant-garde starts to challenge the fixed linguistic code when the imaginary—the symbolic and the poetic imagination—enters art. The symbolic adds a level of depth and the poetic a certain thickness of meaning. The avant-garde becomes a question of life or death; the functional, rigid language is considered, as Lefebvre states, borrowing from Nietzsche, "a harbinger of death." Poetic language is the means of escape for Nietzsche because "poetry consists in a metamorphosis of·signs. In the course of a struggle which overcomes the antagonism between work and play, the poet snatches words from the jaws of death. In the chain of signifiers, he substitutes life for death, and 'decodes' on this basis." [6]

The belief that art can make a difference is supported by Johann Schulte-Sasse in his essay "Theory of Modernism versus Theory of the Avant-Garde." Schulte-Sasse discusses the possibility of a new avant-garde. He criticizes the pessimism of Adorno and Derrida, who see no possibility of a correspondence between art and society, concluding that the subject has somehow lost control as a producer of any meaning. Schulte-Sasse maintains that the subjection of the individual to the perils of mass society is not total, but that ". . . if material, unarticulated experiences exist, and if their effect is a psychic tension or contradiction of some kind, then different degrees of verbal approximation and, thus, of conscious understanding *are possible*." [7] He bases his criticism on the idea of constructed consciousness, which is reflective rather than eternally unaltered, and can therefore be receptive to art that on its part is sensitive to cultural and social developments. "Consciousness rather is the historically concrete production of meaning that *approximates* an accurate articulation of sensuous-material experiences." [8] Similarly, by emphasizing material-sensuous experience, Austria's new avant-garde culture sought to transform consciousness by reassessing experience. Expansion of our views of the real and of meaning in art and architecture is the ultimate goal.

The question in the process of reassessing the avant-garde becomes one of how the material-sensuous experience that allows the "freedom for" is to occur. Schulte-Sasse mentions the slippage between language and ideology. Referring to Bürger and Benjamin, he supports a return to the lost ambiguity between language [architecture?] and experience promoted by the surrealists. This ambiguity forces language to go beyond the epistemological questions of validity and meaning, recalling Artaud's previously discussed theory of natural language, through which the avant-garde can be reconstituted. Peter Bürger writes:

Starting from the experience that a society organized on the basis of a means-ends rationality increasingly restricts the individual's scope, the Surrealists attempt to discover elements of the unpredictable in daily life. Their attention is therefore directed toward those phenomena that have no place in a society that is organized according to the principle of means-ends rationality. The discovery of the marvelous in the everyday undoubtedly constitutes an enrichment of the experiential possibilities of "urban man." But it requires a behavioral type that renounces specific goals in favor of a pervasive openness to impressions.[9]

To secure the momentary existence—the slippage—outside ideology and language, the avant-garde starts to define itself against abstraction and classicism, because they follow a fixed code based on completeness and harmony. Modernist abstraction is opposed, especially its inherent aesthetization, wherein an art work is conceived as a totality, transforming form into content. Classicism becomes the main opponent. Otto Mauer identifies this enemy and defines the opposed strategy of the incomplete, which emphasizes the existential dimension based on real time and place:

I think, that it has taken a very long time in the history of art and the Western spirit to free man from all classicism, from the canonical, that is to say from that which is complete, and what presents that which should exist, not that which already does exist. But this man, who shows his work here, is what one could call a gothicist, a realist, not a classicist. He is interested in the factual, in existence. It is not the substance, the nature, the philosophical, and permanent proposition that is eternally valid, or the proposition that seizes the essence of things and the human being, that interests him, but, rather, the situation; he says nothing about the eternal in man.[10]

It is hardly accidental that Joseph Beyus becomes an emblematic figure in all that Mauer and the new avant-garde strives for. Mauer emphasizes the situational and temporal dimensions of this new realist art. Later he criticizes the modern demand for dominance over nature and calls attention to the accidental and fragile condition of human existence. Instead of eternal symbols such as geometry and harmony, Mauer calls for "transitory symbols": "They are signs for the human condition, for our accidental human existence."[11]

In this context the baroque heritage is posited as a perfect expression of the human condition. The shift is from emphasis on space (*Kunst des Seins*) (art of being) to emphasis on time *Kunst des Werdens* (art of becoming) (Weisbach). The transitory and temporal dimension of art is understood as being always fragmentary and transformable. This move can be assessed easily in the sphere of aesthetic categories: the shift from classical to the romantic principle, from the ideal and eternal to the real and temporal, is a central notion for all twentieth-century avant-gardes.

Mauer follows the intellectual tradition of Nietzsche, Bergson, Benjamin, Bloch, and Adorno when he implies that the fragmentary—the rup-

Top: Klaus Staeck, *Vorsicht Kunst! (Beware Art!),*
1982

Below: Joseph Beuys, *La Rivoluzione siamo Noi,*
1972

ture—correlates with the truth content of art.[12] The fragmentary condenses
single meaningful elements through which art enters the realm of the poetic,
the symbolic. This art aims at creating moments when "the sensitivity is put
in a state of deepened and keener perception"[13]; moments that imply an artistic experience based on fictive reading, rather than a moment of immediacy.
Here imagination and memory represent those deep layers that simple decoding and passive contemplation can never reach.

The celebration of fragmentation and formlessness is based similarly on
this move away from the idea of an abstract space to that of an existential
space, a space of temporal duration. Compared with earlier avant-gardes, this
is critical. Whereas historical avant-garde movements demanded establishment of highly articulated formal languages (Russian constructivism, machine aesthetics, and functionalism are examples), such formal rigidity is
now considered an obstacle to experience.

The Austrian Connection

In every sense, the year 1945 can be understood as a cultural, social, and
intellectual *Stunde Null* (zero point) in Austrian cultural life. The Second World

Pietro de Pomis, mausoleum, Graz,
1616–

War caused a crisis on both individual and national levels, and thus a need to reposition the role of art in a society suddenly almost devoid of cultural life. Austria found itself in a vacuum. Most of its cultural and intellectual elite had been forced to emigrate, and therefore the specific task for art was to reestablish, even reinvent, a culture and establish it in relation to the world culture. The period of occupation just after the war was thus dominated by a cultural aporia; buildings dating from the period bear witness to this state of disorientation. The historical moment that triggered a repositioning was the declaration of the Austrian government of 1955, which ended occupation and laid foundations for a neutral state.[14]

I believe that the Second World War forced the question about the relationship between art and society. I also maintain that today's architectural culture in Austria, as discussed earlier, still reflects the reassessment of its role and function that started in the late 1950s. The reassessment process must be understood in the historical context marked by the problem of cultural identity. Russell A. Berman's assessment of the relationship between cultural discourse and politics informs my thesis: "Central Europe is no sceptered isle. Culture becomes the substitute, the stand-in for a really-existing political confederation as well as the motivation to bring one into being. This connection partially explains the special role played by cultural intellectuals and literary developments in recent formulations of Central European identity."[15]

The reassessment of the avant-garde is influenced by Austria's own cultural heritage. The baroque, as the most dominant single period in its architectural past, forms the spatial and temporal consciousness of the culture, whereas Jugendstil reflects its symbolical consciousness, "the imagination of depth"[16] that characterizes the Austrian mind. Both are rediscovered and used to redefine cultural identity. Throughout this period Austrian culture sought to establish the categories by which to determine and govern its own cultural identity as well as reassess the modern tradition. As Carl Schorske observes in the introduction to Fin-de-Siècle Vienna, the 1950s were internationally marked by "shifting—or at least broadening—the premises for understanding man and society from the social to the psychological realm."[17] Traces of the cultural heritage "part aristocratic, Catholic, and aesthetic, part bourgeois, legalist, and rationalist"[18] are still embedded in the discourse.

One can also see that the situation is in some ways in tune with the strongest periods of Austria's cultural past: the baroque, Jugendstil, and expressionism were similarly born of moments of ideological rupture and shifts of world view. Austrian culture can in large measure be considered born of such moments of crisis. After the Second World War, as in those previous periods,

art gains a central place in the organization of experience that resulted from
the shift of world views.

I believe that the reassessment of the role of the avant-garde happened
through this relocation of cultural heritage, as well as through the intellectual
climate culminating in the 1960s, which celebrated the libidinal and tried to
repoliticize art in one way or another. I also contend that the attitudes, strategies, and techniques that resulted still prevail in contemporary architecture.
The cultural heritage and intellectual climate of the era can be found both in
the manifestos and works of the architects discussed here: the celebration
of the symbolic and liminal in the organic of Günther Domenig, the Wittgensteinian challenge against language in Helmut Richter's structure-space dualism, and the existential and temporal dimension in Volker Giencke's playful
blurring of boundaries.[19]

Perhaps due to Austria's own cultural heritage and its emphasis on
aesthetization of experience, the discourse does not seem to share the cultural
pessimism that dominated the intellectual climate elsewhere. Whereas, for
example, Adorno and Horkheimer, the main representatives of this pessimistic critical theory, see no possibility for freedom and a nonalienated individual existence, the reassessment in Austria starts from precisely the opposite
assumption: that the role of art was to reconstruct the individual realm that
was lost after the totalitarian Nazi regime. When discussing Austrian culture
in particular, it is important to note that it has traditionally played an important role in the society as an indicator of political transformation processes
and in defining questions of individual and national identity.

As a result of the crisis imposed on the national identity, postwar Austrian art participates actively in international discourse. Since the late 1950s
the emphasis moved from abstraction and composition toward the material
celebration of chance, transitoriness, and creative chaos. Art brut, body art,
fluxus, land art, tachism, situationism, and *Wiener Aktionismus* (Viennese
actionism) are all signs of the movement away from object art toward the
making and perceiving of art as a material and sensuous experience with a
temporal dimension. The main objective is to reconstruct experience, which
requires rejecting art based on contemplation.

The construction of sensuous-material experience and celebration of
anti-structure connects Austrian developments since the 1950s to various international movements. Action painting, which understood the finished work
as an index of painterly action, is the main tendency in the Vienna scene
supported by the *Galerie nächst St. Stephan* (Gallery by St. Stephan). The most
influential international influences were Georges Mathieu and Jackson Pol-

lock. The former was the main theoretician for tachism, which unlike American action painting, emphasizes that the technique is based on a strategy of social resistance. In the following passage Mathieu celebrates the existence outside language and ideology that enables the possibility of such resistance:

In all known societies human behavior is regulated by beliefs and ideologies, built on values, which lie on the existing facts. Art exists first in relation to these, and by becoming universal, cuts off every relationship with the reality. The decisive turn, which has now happened in art, which is prophetic by nature, demands therefore a radical change in the realm of ideas and morals. Lyrical abstraction not only established new modes of expression but also new ways of confronting the world based on a radical questioning of Western dialectics from Aristotle to Derrida! . . . As soon as security takes over and the terror will be gone, we will experience the jubilation of risk; the celebration of existence that ensues will introduce not only new aesthetic, but a new morality and new metaphysic as well.[20]

Mathieu's methods and theories were adapted by the group of informalist painters around the Gallery by St. Stephan (Wolfgang Hollegha, Josef Mikl, Markus Prachensky, and Arnulf Rainer), later to be taken over by the more ecstatic and mystical group of the Viennese actionists (Günter Brus, Hermann Nitsch, Alfons Schilling, and Otto Mühl) who finally rejected easel painting altogether. In this process a special ambiance was created, mystic, even sadistic, where the "deepest layers of the psyche are drawn to the surface" (Nitsch), giving a particular Viennese twist to tachist tendencies.

Generally, the postwar art is dominated by art informel and tachism, which both manifest the will to break away from formal and abstract pictorial language. Consistent with the attitude of the 1960s, the desired freedom for creativity and experience is possible only outside language, in the realm of antistructure. Günter Brus's words hint at this: "Language has lost its way. You can still find it in growling and hissing, in screaming and in swallowing. . . ."[21] Art allows the individual to exist, at least momentarily, outside of language and ideology, recalling Schiller's theory of aesthetics as a Freispielplatz, a site where freedom and experience can occur. The task of any new avant-garde is to prove that such freedom is still possible. Schulte-Sasse believes in this possibility: "It is possible to speak of a sensuous-material experience if an organization of society is inscribed in individuals in a way that is independent of language."[22] He and others concur that outside language and ideologies, such language can at least momentarily take place.

Top, left: Wolfgang Hollegha, *Standing Figure with Handle,* 1959

Middle, left: Arnulf Rainer, *The Blindman's Fear,* 1973

Middle, right: Günter Brus, *Action Ana,* 1964

Below: Hermann Nitsch, *50th Action (24 hours),* 1975

Architecture moves more slowly and more hesitantly in the same direction by first reevaluating of its own modernist heritage. Important for this reevaluation is the question of how Austrian modernism posits itself in relation to the classical. Already the work of its two main representatives during the period between the wars, Ernst Plischke and Josef Frank, who were forced to emigrate, starts to suggest a way out of the canonical, classical strands. Frank's work moves toward the organic, whereas Plischke's later work evolves from functionalist aesthetics toward more floating structures reminiscent of Neutra and Schildler. Right after the war this development faced a backlash. Ernst Hieslmayr and Roland Rainer were heirs to the moderate functionalist stance in the late 1950s and 1960s, whereas Karl Schwanzer opened a way for the visionary architecture to emerge, particularly with his Phillips office building in Vienna in 1965. Significant in this reevaluation is the fact that architects such as Giencke and Richter publicly questioned Loos's authority.

Whereas built architecture lagged behind the development in other arts, the theory of tachism was transported into architectural discourse at a very early state. During "the day of architecture" at the international artist symposium at Seckau Abbey in 1958, Friedensreich Hundertwasser presented what later came to be called the "Mould Manifesto," which criticizes utilitarian architecture by promoting the impure—and the nonfunctional. Hundertwasser understands architecture as something that can transform and integrate with nature, to become a living ruin. He translates tachist methods into architecture as follows: "The great turning point—for painting, absolute tachist automatism—is for architecture absolute uninhabitability, which still lies ahead of us, because architecture limps thirty years behind. . . . Merely to carry a straight line about with one ought to be, at least morally, forbidden. The ruler is a symbol of the new illiteracy. The ruler is the symbol of the new sickness of decadence. . . . The straight line is not a creative, but a reproductive line."[23] Here the mechanistic outlook is opposed to the organic, creative outlook, which sees humanity, nature, and architecture as one continuum. Similar ideas are later promoted by Rainer and Prachensky in their manifesto *Architektur mit Händen* ("Architecture with Hands").

Engaged architecture from the late 1970s on starts to catch up with the development of the art avant-garde of the late 1950s and 1960s. From then on architecture similarly focused on the psychic and temporal dimension, reflecting the intellectual climate dominated by existentialism, phenomenology, Marxism, and the reassessment of the psychoanalytic theory. People who participated actively in the development during the late 1950s are still around and building, but the architects of Giencke's generation were students during

Left: Ernst A. Plischke, row house at the Werkbund-siedlung, Vienna, 1930

Below, left: Josef Frank, Wehtje House, Falsterbo, Sweden, 1936

Below, right: Karl Schwanzer, Philips Building, Vienna, 1965

the 1960s and early 1970s, and started to get their first major commissions only in the early 1980s.

The architectural language of COOP Himmelblau and its rhetoric also derive from action painting. The references are found on several levels: first, on the pictorial level, which celebrates antistructure by breaking the horizontal-vertical order; second, in the emphasis placed on automatism in the design process; and third, on the level of rhetoric, which follows more or less that found in the writings of the Viennese actionists during the early 1960s. Statements such as Alfons Schilling's, "We will defend the creative act, even if we have to turn to the ax or the flamethrower," [24] are examples of the shared rhetoric, and invite comparison with COOP Himmelblau's "Architecture Must Burn." The most obvious influence of action painting is the return to expressionistic and organic forms, which dominated architecture in Graz during the 1970s until the late 1980s in the works of Domenig and Huth, Kada, and Szyzkowitz-Kowalski, as discussed earlier.

Here I have concentrated on the more independent developments of architectural culture that came into their own only during the 1980s. I maintain, though, that a level of continuity exists between postwar artistic

Top, right: Jean Dubuffet, Villa Falbala,
1969–1973

Jean Dubuffet, Villa Falbala, interior

Friedensreich Hundertwasser, Hundertwasser
House, Vienna, 1985

Friedensreich Hundertwasser, *The Hamburg Line,*
Hamburg, 1959 (photo: Witling, Hamburg)

tendencies and contemporary Austrian architectural discourse that shuns
questions of formal language as being secondary to the attitude toward making architecture. I claim that through the experiments with body and performance art architecture started to develop and test ideas of temporality (both
in terms of experience pertaining to the subject as well as to the work, the
object); body-environment relationships (body understood in Merleau-
Ponty's sense as intertwined with, rather than solely existing in, the environment); and responsive, dynamic structures. All are ideas that are relevant to
understanding contemporary architectural sensitivity. In some cases the
transport from happenings into architecture was more or less simultaneous.
While COOP Himmelblau and Haus-Rucker-Co experimented with pneumatic structures during the late 1960s in their happenings, Domenig and
Huth were the first to use pneumatic structures in an actual building in their
exhibition pavillion for the Trigon biennal in 1967.

Perhaps the most important shift caused by the move away from abstraction when transported to architecture was the rejection of abstract space in
favor of natural space. The significance of this shift exceeds mere formal question: assumed neutrality is rejected together with compositional strategies of
abstraction. The idea of event-space is engaging, it makes a gesture, it has
character and ambience.

Event-space reassesses architectural experience. Referring to formerly
discussed examples, contemporary architecture has rejected positive space

Haus-Rucker-Co, *Yellow Heart,* 1968
(photo: Gert Winkler)

Günther Domenig and Eilfried Huth, Trigon pavillion, Graz, 1967

based on spatial enclosure and temporal stasis, experience understood as being inside something that characterizes mainstream modernism. Event-space
on the other hand aims to break the (mental) closure of space by denying
the modernist understanding of architecture as space-time. Spatial experience
should never be bound to a single locus, meaning segregation and prohibi-
tion, a body (trapped) in space. Rather, it should transcend spatial boundaries
by means of imagination and active anticipation in what is to come. As
Merleau-Ponty writes, "We have to reject the age-old assumptions that put
the body in the world and the seer in the body, or, conversely, the world and
the body in the seer as in the box." [25] The move away from positive space is
in keeping with the program set for the new avant-garde by Mauer. It is more
about finding an active relationship between humans and the world, of
belonging to the whole, than about an isolated contemplative experience.
Active experience involves anticipation and is therefore by its very nature
temporal rather than cathartic.

The imaginary, the symbolic, and the poetic in art and architecture are
reified in attempts to create endless art objects. The incomplete and the
boundless invite existential readings; the individual and collective, the real
and the imaginary, the inside and outside intermingle. This can be summed
up in Günter Brus's words:

*The possibility of limitless, never-ending painting can only be represented by means of section. How
can I possibly perceive "infinity" in a picture, as long as the possibility of seeing pictures as something
complete in themselves is not removed. Every barrier must be removed from one's own vision (even if
it is only the edge of the picture). Only that which is unstoppable is real painting. A picture must
offer no opportunity of beginning or ending anywhere.* [26]

The concept of the incomplete presents the limit condition of Austrian
postwar avant-garde architecture. The most emblematic project is Frederick
Kiesler's Endless House, which has been copied by several young architects.
First and foremost it marks a shift away from the dialectics of inside and outside. Space is defined by an amorphous skin; it exists both inside and outside
without setting the interior as first priority; only differences of intensities
exist. The Endless House revolutionalized thinking about architectural space.
It created a space that no longer requires us to experience it solely through
its physical presence, but that we can inhabit with our thoughts. It is the
embodiment of the oneiric house of Bachelard, the house of memories and
mental stages. [27]

Top: Constant, *Hanging Sector,* 1960

Middle: Arthur van der Broek, Cafe Rosenheim, competition entry, 1986

Bottom, left: Arnulf Rainer, *Landscape,* 1961

Bottom, right: Markus Prachensky, *Rouges différents,* Gallery St. Stephan, Vienna, 1960 (photo: Barbara Pflaum)

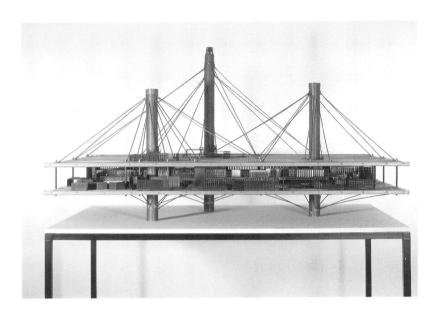

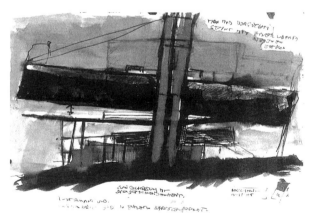

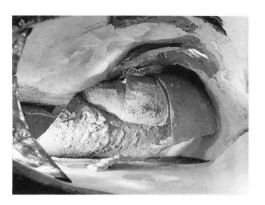

Right: Frederick Kiesler, The Endless House, interior

Middle: Frederick Kiesler, The Endless House, 1959 (photo: Geoffrey Clements Inc., New York 1989)

Bottom, left: Hans Hollein, Stadtskulpturen, Vienna, 1962

Bottom, right: Laurids Ortner, project for an airport, 1964 (photo: Gert Winkler)

The transport of the artistic culture during the 1960s and 1970s into architectural discourse has taken many different forms, and the continuities may not always be as direct as in the examples cited. I find that the search for an imaginary level of architecture, which transcends formal expression, is more relevant to understanding its relationship to the avant-garde tradition than are mere translations of formal, expressive languages. I suggest that tachism taught that architecture should resist the aesthetic approach of formal abstraction that reduces architecture to mere objecthood. Such resistance helps architecture to develop more subtle techniques based on materiality and structure as a way to resist abstraction, spatial closure, and a fixed formal code.

The organic was one way to move beyond the formal and the aesthetic approach of modernism and reach a point at which, as Giencke described it, "the form doesn't really matter." Furthermore I believe that the move away from formal abstraction led to emphasis on materiality and structure. A critic of the *Wiener Aktionismus* wrote, "Viennese actionism can only be explained as a form of excitement towards materials and in actually handling them."[28] The statement also seems valid in relation to Austrian architecture today.

I maintain that key notions, such as the organic, as well as the structural and material emphasis, have run counter to traditional perceptual strategies based on the hierarchical subject-object relationship and are bound to the heritage of surrealism. Both subject and object go through a process of transformation when architecture enters the realm of imagination and desire: a zero degree of architecture. New perceptual strategies have also helped architecture go beyond a spatial experience based solely on movement and visibility. Visuality and space, the two key concepts of the modernist theory, become blurred when the body equipped with vision is transformed into a desiring subject, and space ceases to be based on the simple dialectic of inside and outside.

In this connection I would like to point to *Situationiste International* (SI), rarely mentioned in connection with the Austrian development, yet parallel to it, as another artistic tendency that might help us to understand better the subtle shift that can be found in the works of Giencke, Kada, and Richter, to name just a few. The situationists can be considered direct heirs of surrealism when they celebrate chance as the ultimate urban experience. Their motive for turning to surrealism is the same as in tachism: to celebrate "subjective freedom in a state of objective unfreedom."[29] Situations are conceived as such momentary states of subjective freedom and form a constitutive element of SI's artistic program.

Top: COOP Himmelblau, *Soft Space,* 1970

Middle: Otto Mühl, Material action no. 30, *Food Test,* 1966

Bottom: Constant, *New Babylon Nord,* 1959

According to Guy Debord, situations were "constructed encounters and creatively lived moments in urban settings, instances that critically transformed everyday life."[30] Such statements as, "Our central idea is that of the construction of situations, that is to say, the concrete construction of momentary ambiances of life and their transformation into a superior passional quality,"[31] and, "We must try to construct situations, that is to say, collective ambiances, ensembles of impressions determining the quality of a moment,"[32] imply that the main aim was to create moods and states of mind. That is, the re-creation of a natural space and the material-sensuous experience that would lead to a nonalienated mode of behavior.

Also, when Debord defines situations as something to do with a passional quality he talks about some kind of encounter. Parallels are drawn to phenomena that lack an exact definition, that are somehow boundless, that know no exact physical locus of measure. Desire, passion, and love all entail certain difficulty in taking possession of the sensation. Similarly, as discussed with respect to the Red Stage, situations were thought of as possible sites for intensifying experience and belonging.

The situationists are important to our discussion because they were the first to translate surrealist ideas of the imaginary to the field of urbanism and architecture, displacing the modernist concept of positive space with an ambiguous concept of situation. The notion of eternal presence, embodied in positive space, is neglected in favor of transitory experiences. To experience something involves a passage of time: experience always has a duration. Debord underline this aspect of architecture as a passage, a journey:

. . . we have to multiply poetic subjects and objects—which are now unfortunately so rare that the slightest ones take on an exaggerated emotional importance—and we have to organize games of these poetic objects among these poetic subjects. This is our entire program, which is essentially transitory. Our situations will be ephemeral, without a future; passageways. The permanence of art or anything else does not enter into our considerations, which are serious. Eternity is the grossest idea a person can conceive of in connection with his acts . . . [33]

Again the classical embodied in the ideal and the eternal is rejected in favor of transitory experiences that take us away from the everyday. What is sought is reminiscent of romantic ecstasy or marginal experience inherent in such a situation.

Another situationist critic, Raoul Vaneigem, is after such romantic rhetoric when he calls situations "revolutionary moments [that] are carnivals in which the individual life celebrates its unification with a regenerated soci-

ety."[34] Situations share the avant-garde anticipation of freedom and nonalienation by introducing play into everyday life. Like ritual, situations celebrate
the simultaneity of private sensuous experience and collective ecstasy of experience. Vaneigem continues, "The eruption of lived pleasure is such that in
losing myself I find myself; forgetting that I exist, I realize myself."[35]

Carnival and ritual are moments when profane, everyday life transforms
itself into a moment of celebration. They are familiar both to the Viennese
actionists and to COOP Himmelblau. Their *Flammenaktion* can be understood
through two references: first, the flame, part of the traditional avant-garde
rhetoric used by the Russian constructivists, and second, as reflecting recent
theories of cultural resistance that emphasize ritual as a point of organizing
the relationship between the individual and society. Anthropologist Viktor
Turner calls this realm liminality, a state of ritual that is marked by simultaneous transcendence and belonging. The ritual according to Turner is always
marked by two poles: the ideological, with its sociomoral connotations, and
the sensory level of individual experience. The antistructural tendencies in
the postwar avant-garde relate to this view of ritual as a site where the individual experience gains a collective dimension.[36]

Architecture as a State of Mind

Contemporary Austrian architecture can be connected to those artistic tendencies of the twentieth century that emphasize the role of the imaginary and
the imagination in modern art: surrealism, situationism, and, more recently,
virtual reality. All mark the elimination of the difference between the real and
the unreal that challenges the traditional dichotomy between reality and its
representation. Like those tendencies, contemporary Austrian architecture
can be located in a discussion that challenges rationality with sensuous-
material experience, abstraction with organic, contemplation with desire, reality with fiction,and finally, individual alienation with celebration of the
communal. My discussion has focused on different techniques and strategies
that emphasize this lost dimension of architectural culture that exceeds the
mere formal dimension.

To go beyond the reality principle, contemporary work, as exemplified
here by the work of Giencke and others, combines different techniques that
reorganize the perception process, first, by extended distancing emphasizing
illusion and fantasy, as in the case of glass architecture and technological mysticism; and second, by eliminating distance altogether through an intensified
sense of materiality and detail. Common to both techniques is concern with
triggering the engaged gaze of anticipation, thereby entering the realm of

active imagination. Bachelard's words come to mind: "How concrete every-thing becomes in the world of the spirit when an object, a mere door, can give images of hesitation, temptation, desire, security, welcome and respect."[37]

The creative imagination gives priority to certain design methods. I have discussed the need for experimentation and,in some cases, for automatism. Experimentation provides a ground for balancing the possibilities of available tools and technologies and their extension through chance and imagination. Fascination with technology must be distinguished from formal experimen-tation, which tends simply to push the methods of representation toward new, presumably shocking areas. Manfredo Tafuri contrasts experimentalism and the avant-garde as follows:

The existence of a deep contradiction between the avant-garde and experimentalism has al-ready been accepted. Avant-gardes are always affirmative, absolutist, totalitarian. They claim pe-remptorily to build a brand new context, taking for granted that their linguistic revolution not only implies but actually "realizes" a social and moral upheaval. When Picasso states "I don't look for, I find," he expresses perfectly the assertive character of the avant-gardes. Those who look for must, more or less, work on existing material, choosing, assembling and disassembling. But avant-gardes ignore existing materials. For them nothing is taken for granted or a priori. Their construc-tive act is radical, with Malevitch's "pure desert" as its symbol.

Experimentalism is, on the contrary, constantly taking apart, putting together, contradicting, provoking languages and syntaxes that are nevertheless accepted as such. Its innovation can be bravely launched towards the unknown, but the launching pad is solidly anchored to the ground. Architec-tural experimental research has all the characteristics of tight-rope walking—the wire might break at any moment; or to leave the metaphor behind, one can always discover how absurd or worn out is the theme taken as a research hypothesis—with the protection of a strong net below.[38]

Tafuri's interpretations of the avant-garde and experimentalism are close to nothingness and desire. The history of the avant-garde should not be traced solely through formal tendencies, such as those of Russian constructivism and de Stijl, for the principle of experimentation, of desire, can be found in surrealism, Dada, and expressionism. Even though the works and strate-gies presented in this book are closer to Tafuri's concept of experimentation than those Tafuri claims to belong to the avant-garde, I want to avoid seeing them as competing by pushing the avant-garde toward what Tafuri calls experimentation.

Rather than accepting nothingness as still tied to the reality principle, experimental architecture by its very nature tries to extend reality. Therefore it can be understood as representing the utopian impulse in the work. In

Bloch's terms, it is a discovery of the possible within the real. Blochian ontology is important for this utopian aspiration: truth is not measured by facts but through potentiality embedded in the real. Experimentation releases that latency.[39]

The ultimate goal of these tendencies is to extend architecture beyond the visual and the merely physical; recalling the situationist connection of momentary ambiances with passional quality, the limit condition of the new avant-garde is to turn architecture into a state of mind. To do this architecture must exceed the linguistic and the rational. Again we must make a distinction between the simple dichotomies of meaning and nonmeaning. Rather than leaping into a romantic ecstasy characterized by total negation of language, which ended up being the final blow of Viennese actionism in the 1970s, the new avant-garde strives toward greater ambiguity, heterogeneity, and the elimination of fixed reading.

In opposition to the dichotomy between closure and total disclosure often found in classical modernism, the event-space aims at creating a spatial ambiguity that happens on a phenomenal level. The creation of a certain character and ambiance—architecture as a state of mind—is a prime example of such an ambiguous condition that exists between human beings and the world. Heidegger's definition of disclosure points to this view of spatial ambiguity that goes beyond any literal translation:

The mood has already disclosed, in every case, Being-in the world as a whole, and makes it possible first of all to direct one-self towards something. *Having a mood is not related to the psychical in the first instance, and is not itself an inner condition which then reaches forth in an enigmatical way and puts its mark on things and persons. It is in this that* the second *essential characteristic of states-of-mind shows itself. We have seen that the world, Dasein-with, and existence are equiprimordially disclosed; and state-of-mind is a basic existential species of their disclosedness, because this disclosedness itself is essentially Being in the world.*[40]

The mood is a state of disclosure and therefore a realm between us and the world, and a realm that has an integrating and organizing function. Heidegger continues:

Existentially, a state-of-mind implies a disclosive submission to the world, out of which we can encounter something that matters to us. *Indeed from the ontological point of view we must as a general principle leave the primary discovery of the world to "bare mood." Pure beholding, even if it were to penetrate to the innermost core of the Being of something present-at-hand, could never discover anything like that which is threatening.*[41]

Fredl Bramberger, Tummelplatz, Graz, 1990–
1991 (photo: Paul Ott)

Walter de Maria, *The Lightning Field,* 1977 (photo: John Cliett)

Klaus Kada, apartments by the Stadtpark, Graz, 1991

Equally important is the temporal dimension event-space opens up. A material experience is a zone of possibilities where events take place: "The idea of the possible when, instead of grasping each existent in its novelty, the whole of existence is related to a preformed element, from which everything is supposed to emerge by simple 'realization.'"[42] Each event is understood as a happening, rather than as a new progression toward the ultimate goal. Therefore the event-space is based on a totally different concept of time: mythical circular time instead of linear time. Some sort of static utopia is therefore not the ultimate goal. As Mathieu pointed out, rather than prefiguring the future, art understood as an event, an act, simply opens up to the future.

The utopian function of architecture conceived as a state of mind can be understood through this opening of a field of possibilities. Two basic strategies are explicit: intervention and extension. Architecture as intervention brings the imaginary into the realm of the everyday by extending the scope of experience. The utopian potential of the imaginary, on the other hand, is based on extension of the real itself. Tomás Llorens's question, "whether the field of possibility is larger than that of reality, and this, in turn, larger than that of necessity?"[43] is relevant in this context. Instead of seeing the real and the imaginary as binary opposites, their relationship becomes unstable. Heidegger's concept potentiality for being develops this idea of the opening of possibilities:

As something factical, Dasein's projection of itself understandingly is in each case already alongside a world that has been discovered. From this world it takes its possibilities, and it does so first in accordance with the way things have been interpreted by the "they." This interpretation has already restricted the possible options of choice to what lies within the range of the familiar, the attainable, the respectable—that which is fitting and proper. This levelling of Dasein's possibilities to what is proximately at its everyday disposal also results in a dimming down of the possible as such. The average everydayness of concern becomes blind to its possibilities, and tranquillizes itself with that which is merely "actual." This tranquillizing does not rule out a high degree of diligence in one's concern, but arouses it. In this case no positive new possibilities are willed, but that which is at one's disposal becomes "tactically" altered in such a way that there is a semblance of something happening. All the same, this tranquillized "willing" under the guidance of the "they," does not signify that one's Being toward one's potentiality-for-Being has been extinguished, but only that it has been modified. In such a case, one's Being toward possibilities shows itself for the most part as mere wishing.[44]

I maintain that postwar art and architecture of Austria are based on the realization that it is important to keep the utopian impulse alive, and that these might be the only realms where wishing and dreaming can still find physical expression—*Rausch*.

To keep the utopian impulse alive, the work has to resist picturing the *Ultimum*, the state of crystallization. Bloch's social utopian philosophy retains this mythic project. For him all great art shares this feature of becoming: "Every great work of art thus still remains, except for its manifest character, impelled towards the latency of the other side, i.e. towards the contents of a future which had not yet appeared in its own time, if not towards the contents of an as yet unknown final state."[45] To continue directing toward the future, a utopian project has to be perpetually incomplete and in the process of becoming.

Concrete utopia as object-determination presupposes concrete fragment as object-determination and involves it, even through certainty as an ultimate revocable fragment. And therefore every artistic, and especially every religious pre-appearance is only concrete on the basis and to the extent that the fragmentary in the world ultimately presents the layer and the material for it to constitute itself as pre-appearance.

It is a question of realism, everything real has a horizon.[46]

By rejecting any a priori architectural language, the new avant-garde denies the relevance of formal strategies of the historical avant-gardes, which define themselves through a clear opposition between mainstream and the margin. They take for granted that the former position, or architecture in general, can be defined as easy categorization in the first place. It is understood through multiplicity and incompleteness rather than through the absolute and the complete. It becomes a living condition rather than something to do with composition and form, which always strive for permanence and completion. John Cage, a fellow-traveler of twentieth-century avant-gardes, dreamed of such a condition where art would enter the realm of the living. Gerald L. Bruns discusses Cage's work as such a "living practice" as follows:

Imagine art, or philosophy, not as cognition (not even as "perceptive equilibrium"), but as a way or turning things loose, freeing them . . . Cage's art is like this: not chaotic, not incoherent or unintelligible, but anarchic and unassimilable (unassemblable), not part of design: without why—in the spirit of Meister Eckhart: external to art and philosophy (just the way the world is: intimate, embraceable).[47]

I suggest that contemporary Austrian architecture can be understood in the context of the negative informed by phenomenology and Christian mythology, as well as the anarchic philosophies of antistructure allowing the letting loose of things. I believe that the new avant-garde is exactly based this ethos of anarchic incompleteness that blurs distinctions and merges tendencies, seeing them not as isolated formal strategies but synthesized into a kind of living tradition where communication occurs. Architecture as a state of mind sees things through the collapse of otherness striving for an idea of a new community, of new beginning, similar to the Cagean letting loose of things.

The negative element that guarantees incompletion is evident through obtrusiveness, fragmentation, and negation of spatial integrity. The event-space—architecture happening in real time and place, triggering anticipation and engagement—is an attempt to open architecture to the imaginary and the possible. The event becomes an embodiment of such extensions of the real as moments of intensified sense of being alive. Merleau-Ponty sums it up:

> . . . it is necessary to incorporate into being a whole quantity of negative attributes, the transitions, and the becoming, and the possible. As always the same negativist thought oscillates between these two images without being able to sacrifice one of them nor to unite them. It is ambivalence itself, that is, the absolute contradiction and the identity of being and nothingness, it is the "ventiriloquial" thought that Plato speaks of, that which always affirms or denies in the hypothesis what it denies or affirms in the thesis, that which as high-altitude thinking belies the inherence of being in nothingness and of nothingness in being.[48]

What's Love Got to Do With It? (Epilogue)

What I have called the new avant-garde can be distinguished from the historical avant-garde by a special kind of sentiment and pathos inherent in the work that is antithetical to understanding the avant-garde as having a critical position in the society. It is exactly the ability to create an ambience that marks the difference between two possible understandings. I believe that it is gesture and ambience, in the case of the Red Stage, for example, of intimacy and yearning, that make the difference between good and bad (architecture) politics.

The difference lies in how the cognitive project is reassessed. The strategies of the critical avant-garde are based on the transgression of architectural language, which results in turning architecture into a self-conscious formal practice. The new avant-garde, on the other hand, relies on the transgression of form based on the enhancement of material presence leading to the creation of an ambience; form really does not matter. I believe that this architecture as a state of mind participates in the reassessment of the avant-garde project by continuing a latent surrealist heritage prevailing in twentieth-century intellectual and artistic culture.

Volker Giencke, Kepler gymnasium, Graz, 1990–
1992, entrance and toplights of the underground
gymnastic hall

This is where love enters our discussion. Benjamin understood love as being such a forcefield that it could well serve the revolution. He discusses this radical notion of love through André Breton's Nadja.

. . . one need only take love seriously to recognize in it, too—as Nadja also indicates—a "profane illumination." . . . We have from a recent author quite exact information on Provençal love poetry, which comes surprisingly close to the Surrealist conception of love.

Benjamin continues by quoting Erich Auerbach:

All the poets of the "new style" possess a mystical beloved, they all have approximately the same very curious experience of love; to them all Amor bestows or withholds gifts that resemble an illumination more than sensual pleasure; all are subject to a kind of secret bond that determines their inner and perhaps also their outer lives.[49]

The surrealists sought to enhance moments of intensity, where mere sensuous pleasure, that is, the classical principle, is rejected for the operational pleasure of intensified energy of the romantic principle. Love radicalizes the cognitive project by mediating between physical reality as a pregiven condition and the potentiality latent in that condition, while seeking out the utopian impulse in the real.

I suggest a similar strategy for the new avant-garde. By transgressing mere physical reality, both love and architecture find their sites in imagination and phantasm. Giorgio Agamben discusses the quality of phantasm as the locus of desire:

Indeed, the phantasm, which is the true source of desire ("phantasia ea est, quae totum parit desiderium"), is also—mediator between man and object—the condition for attainability of the object of desire and therefore, ultimately, for desire's satisfaction. . . . It is precisely because here love is not the opposition between a desiring subject and an object of desire but has in the phantasm, so to speak, its subject-object, that the poets can define its character (in contrast with a fol amour which can only consume its object without ever being truly with it, without ever experiencing it) as a fulfilled love . . . whose delight never ends.[50]

I suggest that by resisting the object-character of architecture, the peripheral views of the new avant-garde trigger imagination and desire, which eliminate the distance between subject and object in favor of a more direct correspondence. Thus liminal architecture becomes a phantasm that occupies a mediative role between subject and object, reality and potentiality. Rather than being based on language, phantasm makes communication enter into

Bureau des Rèscherches Surréalistes, *If you love
LOVE you'll love SURREALISM* (1924–1928)

the realm of something much more subtle, an intermediate zone that is the
abode of thought and imagination. Whereas language operates on the level
of consciousness, imagination and thought are marked by indecisiveness and
doubt, having the character of a hunch.

This in-between realm of imagination and thought can also be found in
the surrealist sensibility that aimed at the unity and belonging inherent in the
condition of being in love. I suggest that it is in the light of this heritage, love
and surrealism, that the works previously discussed should be talked about.
Paul Mann describes the surrealist condition of in-between as follows:

*In surrealism three is uncountable. Everywhere the surrealist looks, the world is organized in twos,
in amorous or warring pair, like beasts lining up to escape the flood. Surrealism is a mania for the
binary: reason and madness, mundane reality and dreamed ideal, logic and objective chance: it is
always a matter of combination, of opposition, of the real and the anti and some hope for their future
resolution in the absolute surreal.*[51]

The emblematic condition of the binary can, as surrealists themselves
understood very well, be found in love and in eroticism. Love, eroticism,
and also, I suggest, engaged architecture—the event-space—occur in the in-
between zone characterized by blurring of boundaries, heightened sense of
temporality, and moments marked by chance and change. It is the simultaneous collapse and acknowledgment of difference that constitutes desire.
Mann continues:

*There is, first of all, the erotic encounter. . . . surrealism wants to eliminate the distinction between
these encounters, between what one loves and what one imagines, between what one desires and what
one is. . . . The eroto-imaginative encounter is always riven by some difference; its truth is gauged
by the intensity of the difference it embraces.*[52]

So, what does love have to do with architecture? I believe that essentially
it is a question of separating the dead from the living. Reminiscent of the
condition of being in love, which makes us approach life through exceptions
rather than through the norm, architecture as a state of mind can be understood as a more peripheral and liminal condition than as a formal practice.
Just like when we are in love we recognize the thin line that separates life
from death, and that to be living is an exception rather than a rule, architecture as a state of mind—the new avant-garde?—characterized by peripheral
concepts, and presents itself as a fragile condition. Such fragile conditions
makes us realize what constitutes architecture in the first place; the moment
architecture happens is in fact an exception rather than a normative condition. A new utopia!

Steirischer Herbst, poster, 1993

Asger Jorn, *Vive la Revolution Pasioné,* poster,
1968

Steirischer Akademie, *LOVE (Big Feelings),* poster,
1993

Notes

Introduction

1. See recent criticism of the Western metaphysical tradition, for example, in Gilles Deleuze and Felix Guattari, *Anti-Oedipus: Capitalism and Schizophrenia* (New York: Viking Press, 1977), or in Fredric Jameson, *The Political Unconscious: Narrative as a Socially Symbolic Act* (Ithaca, NY: Cornell University Press, 1981).

2. Michel Foucault in his introduction to Deleuze and Guattari's *Anti-Oedipus*, xi.

3. R. D. Laing's *The Politics of Experience* (New York: Pantheon Books, 1967) informs my reassessment of architectural experience, Laing challenges the traditional dichotomy between behavior and experience, that is, inner and outer experience. He does this by decentralizing experience through the emphasis he puts on imagination, dreams, and fantasy. He writes, "The way that my experience is intrapsychic is to presuppose that there is a psyche that my experience is in. My psyche is my experience, my experience is my psyche" 7.

4. Ernst Bloch's *Das Prinzip Hoffnung* (Frankfurt: Surkamp, 1959) has been an important point of reference both in terms of architectural discourse in postwar Europe, as well as in understanding the intellectual culture in the German-speaking area after the war. Bloch played an important role in the student movement in Germany during the 1970s. I consider the dialogue between him and Adorno particularly relevant to my discussion. See also Theodor W. Adorno's "Functionalism Today," in *Oppositions* 17 (New York: Institute for Architecture and Urban Studies, 1977).

5. Foucault states this question in the introduction to Deleuze and Guattari's *Anti-Oedipus* as follows: "How does one introduce desire into thought, into discourse, into action?", xii.

6. Henri Lefebvre, *The Production of Space* (Cambridge: Basil Blackwell, 1991), 99.

7. Deleuze and Guattari, *Anti-Oedipus*, 25.

8. Roland Barthes, *Writing Degree Zero* (Boston: Beacon Press, 1967), 44–45.

9. Giorgio Agamben, *The Coming Community* (Minneapolis: University of Minnesota Press), 41.

10. Here I have been also informed by Jameson's idea of "the political unconscious" and Laing's theory of the "ego-loss." Jameson enhances the collective as follows: "Marxian interpretation must anticipate in conceiving those new forms of collective thinking and collective culture which lie beyond the boundaries of our own world," 11.

11. Barthes, *Writing Degree Zero*, 9.

12. Ibid., 13–14.

13. Friedrich Achleitner, "Mit und gegen Hauberrisser?—Einige Behauptungen zu 'Grazer Schule'" from *Architektur aus Graz* (Graz, 1981), 6 (my translation). (*Der Ausbruch der sechziger Jahre hat ganz bestimmte Merkmale. Graz hat schneller, heftiger und auch bedingungsloser (unkritischer?) auf internationale Tendenzen reagiert.*)

14. A major figure in the development has been *Hofrat* Wolfdieter Dreibholz, a leading civil servant at the department of housing and public works in the provincial government. He acted as a mediator between architects and the provincial government,

and in many ways can be called the mastermind behind the role that architecture was to assume in local politics since the late 1970s.

15. The vivid architectural scene in Graz today is to a great extent due to the extensive competition program regulated by the local government. For example, in the case of a housing project of more than twenty-five units, a limited competition is required; in the case of more than fifty units, an open competition has to be held. During 1990–1991 more than fifty competitions were held annually in Styria alone. Since then the number has gone down due to changes in the political power structure of the local government. Architects now fear a regressive turn in local politics.

Chapter 1

1. Antonin Artaud, *Collected Works* 2 (London: Calder & Boyars, 1974), 210.

2. Antonin Artaud, *Collected Works* 4 (London: Calder & Boyars, 1974), 64.

3. Ibid., 65.

4. Paul Mann, *Theory Death of Avant-Garde* (Bloomington: Indiana University Press, 1991), 94.

5. Kenneth Frampton, "Towards a Critical Regionalism," in *Post-Modern Culture* (also known as *The Anti-Aesthetics*), Hal Foster, Ed. (London: Pluto Press, 1988), 16–30. Opposing Giedeon's oculocentrism, Frampton develops the idea of tactile vision based on the "complementary sensory perceptions which are registered by the labile body," 28.

6. Michael Hays, *Modernism and the Post-Humanist Subject; the Architecture of Hannes Mayer and Ludwig Hilberseimer* (Cambridge: MIT Press, 1991), 18.

7. Ibid., 19–20.

8. Cf. Colin Rowe and Robert Slytzky, "Transparency: Literal and Phenomenal," in Colin Rowe, *Mathematics of the Ideal Villa and Other Essays* (Cambridge: MIT Press, 1976). Rowe and Slytzky's essay is a key text in this context. Based exactly on this idea of perceptual fallacy, it discusses the relationship between the image as a representation and the real as its referent. The article demonstrates the understanding of phenomenal pertaining to mere appearance common in Anglo-American philosophy. Continental philosophy on the other hand emphasizes that perception happens within the world rather than external to it, whereas Rowe and Slytzky's readings of Villa Stein are reminiscent of Plato's dictum that man is perpetually trapped in the cave looking at shadows. The dimension of time is therefore excluded in the positivist Anglo-American philosophical tradition, whereas it is an essential part of continental philosophy.

9. Hays, *Modernism*, 154.

10. Gilles Deleuze, *Cinema 2; Time-Image* (Minneapolis: University of Minnesota Press, 1989), 17.

11. Ibid., xi.

12. Gaston Bachelard, *The Poetics of Space* (Boston: Beacon Press, 1969), p. 219.

13. Deleuze, *Cinema 2*, 22.

14. Roland Barthes, *Elements of Semiology* (New York: Hill & Wang, 1968), 39.

15. Maurice Merleau-Ponty, *Phenomenology of Perception* (New York: Routledge & Kegan Paul, 1962), 28.

16. Ibid., 29.

17. Deleuze, *Cinema 2*, 125.

18. Hays, *Modernism*, 17.

19. Giorgio Agamben, *Coming Community* (Minneapolis: University of Minnesota Press, 1993), 43.

20. Martin Heidegger, "The Origin of the Work of Art," in *Poetry, Language, Thought* (New York: Harper & Row, 1975), 46.

21. Agamben, *Coming Community*, 35–36.

22. Ibid., 36.

23. Octavio Paz, *Marcel Duchamp; Appearance Stripped Bare* (New York: Viking Press, 1978), 28.

24. Cf. Gilles Deleuze, *Cinema 2*, glossary. See also the discussion about "Nooschock" 15. What I call the muteness of the image is very much informed by Deleuze's idea of the time-image. Deleuze writes, "time-image puts thought into contact with an unthought, the unsummonable, the inexplicable, the undecidable, the incommensurable," 214.

25. Ibid., 169.

26. Merleau-Ponty, *Phenomenology of Perception*, 182.

27. See Karsten Harries, "Transformations of the Subjunctive," in *Thought* (September 1980), 285. Harries quotes Aristotle's *Poetics*: "Poets function is to describe not the thing that has happened but a kind of thing that might happen, i.e., what is possible as being probable or necessary."

28. Jean-Luc Godard, *Godard on Godard* (New York: Viking Press, 1972), 213.

29. The following dialogue between Godard and an interviewer from *Cahiers du Cinema* demonstrates the same sensitivity:

    Cahiers: There is a good deal of blood in Pierrot [*le Fou*].

    Godard: Not blood, red.

30. Godard's films are often interpreted as being based on montage and fragmentation. The following passage is relevant for understanding the temporal and atmospheric quality of his use of image: "The interesting thing is this sort of fluidity, being able to feel existence like physical matter: it is not the people who are important, but the atmosphere between them. Even when they are in close-up, life exists around them." See "Let's Talk about Pierrot," in *Godard on Godard*, 211–212.

31. Bernice Martin, *A Sociology of Contemporary Cultural Change* (Oxford: Basil Blackwell, 1981), 99.

32. Georg Simmel quoted by Beatriz Colomina, "Adolf Loos and Josef Hofmann; Architecture in the Age of Mechanical Reproduction," in *Raumplan versus Plan Libre* (New York: Rizzoli, 1991), 65.

33. Heidegger, "The Origin of the Work of Art," in *Poetry*, . . . , 83.

34. Massimo Cacciari, *Architecture of Nihilism* (New Haven: Yale University Press, 1993), xxv.

35. Agamben, *Coming Community*, 53–56.

36. Deleuze, *Time-Image*, 170.

37. Cf. Deleuze, "What Is an Event?," in *The Fold* (Minneapolis: University of Minnesota Press, 1993), 76–82.

38. Godard, *Godard on Godard*, 218.

39. Julia Kristeva, *Revolution in Poetic Language* (New York: Columbia University Press, 1984), 99–100.

40. Agamben, *Coming Community*, 54.

41. Ibid., 56.

42. Michel Foucault, "Of Other Spaces," in *Diacritics* (Spring 1986), 24.

43. Ibid., 24.

44. Foucault describes the other spaces as "a sort of simultaneously mythic and real contestation of the space in which we live, this description could be called heterotopy."

45. Agamben, *Coming Community*, 1.

Chapter 2

1. Wolfgang Prix and Helmut Swiczinsky quoted by Günter Feuerstein, *Visionäre Architektur Wien 1958–88* (Vienna: Löcker Verlag, 1980), 210. Peter Blundell-Jones translated the manifesto somewhat clumsily as follows: "We want architecture that has more. We want architecture which bleeds, which exhausts, which revolves and breaks. An architecture which shines, which stings, shreds and splits apart while revolving. When cold then as cold as an iceblock, when hot then as hot as a wing of flame. Architecture must burn," in "The New Spirit," *Architectural Review* no. 1074, (August 1986).

2. Martin Heidegger, *On the Way to Language* (Pfüllingen: Verlag Günter Neske, 1975), 179.

3. Ibid., 181.

4. Cf. Heidegger's discussion on potentiality-for-Being, in *Being and Time* (New York: Harper & Row, 1962), 279–281.

5. Cf. Jean-Paul Sartre, chapter 2, "The Look," in *Being and Nothingness* (New York: Philosophical Library, 1956).

6. Maurice Merleau-Ponty, *Phenomenology of Perception* (New York: Routledge & Kegan Paul, 1962), 324. "A thing," unlike the object, is something that belongs to "nature" and is therefore "alien" to humans.

7. Cf. Karsten Harries, "Light Without Love," in *The Broken Frame* (Washington, D.C.: The Catholic University Press, 1989), 1–32.

8. In this context I refer both to Venturi's famous dictum "less is a bore" and to Hans Hollein's manifesto "Everything Is Architecture," in *Architecture Culture 1943–1968*,

Joan Ockman, Ed. (New York: Columbia Books of Architecture, 1993), 360.

9. Sadie Plant, *The Most Radical Act: A Situationist International in a Post-Modern Age* (London: Routledge & Kegan Paul, 1992), 62.

10. Merleau-Ponty, *Phenomenology of Perception*, 154.

11. Ibid., 211.

12. Quoted by Sadie Plant, *The Most Radical Act*, 20.

13. Volker Giencke, *Architektur—Investitionen; Grazer "Schule" 13 Standpunkte* (Graz: Akademische Druck- und Verlagsanstalt, 1986), 18.

14. Here I refer to the discussion of Giencke's work in Peter Cook, *The New Spirit in Architecture* (New York: Rizzoli, 1991), 116–119.

15. David Sylvester, *The Brutality of Fact: Interviews with Francis Bacon* (London: Thames & Hudson, 1975), 63.

16. *Wiener Aktionismus* can be understood as a culmination of the *Informel* tendencies of postwar European art. Their art actions are characterized by excessive bodily exposure and blurring of religious mysticism with orgiastic themes. The main members of the group that existed in the late 1960s were Günter Brus, Otto Mühl, Hermann Nitsch, and Robert Schwartzkugel. See *Von Aktionsmalerei zum Aktionismus 1960–1971* (Klagenfurt: Ritter Verlag, 1989); *Wiener Aktionismus 1960–1965* (Klagenfurt: Ritter Verlag, 1988); and Robert Fleck, *Avant-Garde in Wien: Die Geschichte der Galerie St. Stephan Wien 1954–1982; Kunst und Kunstbetrieb in Österreich* (Vienna: Löcker Verlag, 1982). See also the last chapter, "The New Avant-Garde?", for a further discussion on the relation between artistic culture and architectural discourse in postwar Austria.

17. Cf. Robert Smithson's essay, "Frederick Law Olmsted and the Dialectical Landscape," in *Writings of Robert Smithson*, Nancy Holt, Ed. (New York: New York University Press, 1979), 117–128.

18. Jurgis Baltrušaitis's definition of anamorphosis (also called "depraved" or "curious perspectives") is useful in this context. On the title page of *Aberrations: An Essay on the Legend of Forms* (Cambridge: MIT Press, 1989) he gives the following description: "The optical depravations known as anamorphoses and aberrations (in astronomical sense), which, by allowing things to be seen other than as they are, have given rise, *vis-à-vis* sight, to legends of forms and *vis-à-vis* the mind, to the legends of myth. They are all the product of the same logical and poetical mechanism."

19. Gilles Deleuze, *Cinema 2; Time-Image* (Minneapolis: University of Minnesota Press, 1989), 189.

20. Roland Barthes, *The Pleasure of the Text* (New York: Hill & Wang, 1975), 17.

21. See Peter Wollen, "Bitter Victory: The Art and Politics of the Situationist International," in *On the Passage of a Few People Through a Rather Brief Moment in Time, The Situationist International 1957–1972*, Elisabeth Sussman, Ed. (Cambridge: MIT Press, 1989), 44. The Situationist International was an international avant-garde group gathered around the film maker-critic Guy Debord from the late 1950s to the early 1970s. Their artistic agenda was based on the critique of alienation as described by Henri Lefebvre. The situationists had a strong agenda for architecture and urbanism; cre-

ated situations would provide moments of a heightened sense of belonging. See Ken Knabb, Ed., *Situationist International Anthology* (Berkeley, CA: Bureau of Public Secrets, 1981); Sadia Plant, *The Most Radical Act*, Elisabeth Sussman Ed., *On the Passage*. . . . For a further discussion, see also "Architecture as a State of Mind" in chapter 4.

22. *Dérive* was one of the key concepts in situationist theory. According to Jorn it means simply "drift down the city street." His definition also implies an element of game and play. See Asger Jorn, "Unitary Urbanism at the End of 50s," in Sussman, *On the Passage . . .* , 134.

23. Gilles Ivain quoted in Elisabeth Sussman's introduction to *On the Passage . . .* , 9. In *Megastructure; Urban Futures of the Recent Past* (New York: Harper & Row, 1979) Reyner Banham gives a similar description to Constant's Neo-Babylone project: "The vast structures in the mode of urbanisme spatiale as far as their frameworks were concerned were intended paradoxically to support the lightest of human activities—urban life viewed as the playing out of an open game, giant playgrounds for *Homo ludens.*"

24. Slavoj Žižek, *An Introduction to Jacques Lacan through Popular Culture* (Cambridge: MIT Press, 1991), 4.

25. Ibid., 5.

26. Ibid., 6.

27. Ibid., 11–12.

28. Paul Scheerbart quoted by Iain Boyd Whyte, *Bruno Taut and the Architecture of Activism* (Cambridge: MIT Press, 1982), 180 (my translation). ("In style the play is the goal. In play the goal is the style. At goal the play is the style.")

29. Raoul Vaneigem quoted by Sadie Plant, *The Most Radical Act*, 73.

30. Cf. Kant's discussion on space in the *First Critique of Pure Reason*, 67–74.

31. Quoted in Mark Poster, *Existential Marxism; From Sartre to Althusser* (Princeton: Princeton University Press, 1975), 91.

32. Antonin Artaud, *Collected Works* 4 (London: Calder & Boyars, 1971), 64–65.

33. Roger Connah, *Writing Architecture: Fantômas, Fragments, Fictions; an Architectural Journey Through the 20th Century* (Cambridge: MIT Press, 1989), 147.

34. Barthes, *The Pleasure of the Text*, 57.

35. Herbert Marcuse, *Eros and Civilization* (Boston: Beacon Press, 1955), 65.

36. Ernst Bloch, *The Principle of Hope* (Cambridge: MIT Press, 1986). Vol. 2, 701.

37. Le Corbusier, *The City of Tomorrow* (Cambridge: MIT Press, 1971), 11.

38. Connah, *Writing Architecture*, 148.

39. Ibid., 149.

40. Barthes, *The Pleasure of the Text*, 4.

41. Roland Barthes, *Image, Music, Text* (New York: Farrar, Strauss & Giroux, 1977), 157.

42. Barthes, *The Pleasure of the Text*, 7.

43. Ibid., 10.

44. Richard Rorty, *Philosophy and the Mirror of Nature* (Princeton: Princeton University Press, 1979), 372.

45. Cf. Susan Buck-Morss, *The Dialectics of Seeing; Walter Benjamin and the Arcades Project* (Cambridge: MIT Press, 1989), 129–130.

46. Paul Scheerbart, *Glass Architecture* (New York: Praeger Publishers, 1972), 72.

47. Here I refer to Reyner Banham's comment that glass architecture represents "the aseptic side of modern architecture." See his *Theory and Design in the First Machine Age* (London: Architectural Press, 1960), 266.

48. James Farlane, "The Mind of Modernism," in *Modernism*, Malcolm Bradbury and James McFarlane, Ed. (London: Penguin Books, 1985), 71. (*Heute scheinen zwei Dinge modern zu sein: die Analyse des Lebens und die Flucht aus dem Leben . . . Man treibt Anatomie des eigenen Seelenlebens, oder man träumt. Reflexion oder Phantasie, Spiegelbild oder Traumbild.*)

49. Cf. Georg Simmel, "Metropolis and Mental Life," in *Georg Simmel: On Individuality and Social Forms* (Chicago: University of Chicago Press, 1985).

50. See Buck-Morss's chapter, "Mythic Nature: Wish Image," in *The Dialectics of Seeing*, 110–158.

51. Ibid., 116.

52. Giorgio Agamben, *Stanzas; Word and Phantasm in Western Culture* (Minneapolis: University of Minnesota Press, 1993), 42–43.

53. Ibid., 42–43.

54. Birgit Pelzer, "Vision in Process," in *October 10* (Fall 1979), 115. Here Pelzer participates in the discussion that started to reassess vision and criticize Western oculo-centrisim in the end of the 1970s using psychoanalytic methods. The following sentence sums up her argument: "Vision, naturally associated with the order of consciousness, (witness the triumph of geometrical perspective contemporaneous with Descartes' postulates), belongs less to that order than that of desire."

55. Dominique G. Laporte, *Christo* (New York: Pantheon Books, 1986), 28.

56. Elaine Scarry, *The Body in Pain: The Making and Unmaking of the World* (Oxford: Oxford University Press, 1985), 285.

57. Paul Virilio, "The Overexposed City," in *The Lost Dimension* (New York: Semiotext(e), 1991), 17.

Chapter 3

1. Adolf Loos, "Ornament and Crime," in Ulrich Conrads, *Programs and Manifestos on 20th-Century Architecture* (Cambridge: MIT Press, 1991), 20.

2. Here I refer to COOP Himmelblau's "Architektur muß brennen," in Günter Feuerstein, *Visionäre Architektur Wien 1958–88* (Berlin: Ernst & Sohn, 1988), 210.

3. Friedrich Nietzsche, *The Birth of Tragedy and the Case of Wagner* (New York: Random House, 1967), 22.

4. Loos, Ornament and Crime, 20.

5. Theodor W. Adorno, "Functionalism Today," *Oppositions* 17 (summer 1979): 35.

6. Here I refer to Adorno's lecture, "Functionalism Today," in *Oppositions* 17 (1977), 31–58, and Bloch's essay "Creation of an Ornament," in *The Utopian Function of Art and Literature: Selected Essays* (Cambridge: MIT Press, 1989), 78–102.

7. Loos, *Ornament and Crime*, 23.

8. I refer to Lefebvre's *The Production of Space* (Cambridge: MIT Press, 1989). See especially his discussion on page 34, where he states: "Like all social practice, spatial practice is lived directly before it is conceptualized; but the speculative primacy of the conceived over the lived causes practice to disappear along with life, and so does very little justice to the 'unconscious' level of lived experience." The lived is supposed to allow an immediacy not unsimilar to an image, which condenses rather than separates different levels of information and meaning.

9. Loos eliminated the discussion about the production of architecture and forms by believing that "forms cannot be invented," but appear "spontaneously" due to the devine power of "genius." See Yehuda Safran, "The Curvature of the Spine; Krauss, Loos and Wittgenstein" in *9H*, no. 4 (1983).

10. Adorno, "Functionalism Today," p. 37.

11. Cf. Kenneth Frampton, "Towards a Critical Regionalism," in *Post-Modern Culture*, Hal Foster, Ed. (London: Pluto Press, 1985), 16–30.

12. Cf. Martin Heidegger, "The Origin of a Work of Art," in *Poetry, Language, Thought* (New York: Harper & Row, 1975), 15–87.

13. Ernst Bloch, *The Principle of Hope*, 87.

14. Susan Buck-Morss, *The Dialectics of Seeing* (Cambridge: MIΓ Press, 1991), 220. She discusses Benjamin's idea of "the dialectical image" as follows: "it allows the superimposition of fleeting images present and past, made both suddenly come alive in forms."

15. For Benjamin, fragment gains importance as "a progressive form" that "counteracts illusion" and breaks the false consciousness of art. See Buck-Morss, *The Dialectics of Seeing*, 67.

16. Theodor W. Adorno, *Aesthetic Theory* (London: Routledge & Kegan Paul, 1984), 128.

17. Lefebvre, *The Production of Space*, 176–177.

18. Walter Benjamin, *Reflections* (New York: Schocken Books, 1969), 179.

19. Lefebvre, *The Production of Space*, 97.

20. Ibid., 99.

21. Fredric Jameson quoted by David Harvey, *The Condition of Postmodernity* (Cambridge: Blackwell Publishers, 1993), 54.

22. Cicero quoted by Frances Yates, *The Art of Memory* (London: Routledge & Kegan Paul, 1966), 10. Ioan P. Couliano in *Eros and Magic in the Renaissance* (Chicago: University of Chicago Press, 1987) attributes *Ad Herennium* to St. Thomas, 33.

23. Gilles Deleuze, *Thousand Plateaus* (London: Anthone Press Ltd., 1988), 172. Deleuze later develops this notion of lost distance to the idea of haptic vision: "Where there is close vision, space is not visual, or rather the eye itself has a haptic, nonoptical function . . .", 494.

24. The facade for Loos was a divider between private and public realms. Behind his austere facades one finds sensuous use of material and spatial gestures. The facade of Moller House is emblematic, whereas the interior of American Bar manifests the

material sensitivity of Loos's interior spaces. A similar dichotomy is found in many rococo churches. Here I rely on the examples published in Karsten Harries's *The Bavarian Rococo Church* (New Haven: Yale University Press, 1983).

25. Helmut Richter quoted by Gottfrid Fliedl, "Ausstellen," in *Dichte Packung; Architektur aus Wien*, Otto Kapfinger and Franz E. Kneissl, Ed. (Vienna: Residenz Verlag, 1989), 195. Originally published in *Umbau* 1983/84 (my translation). (*Warum entscheiden wir uns im Bad zum Beispiel nich für Fliesen, sie waren wahrscheinlich billiger; der Spiegel macht den Raum größer, gibt ein anderes Licht—aber ist das ein Argument? Ab hier sollten Argumente wegbleiben, sie werden lächerlich, sie geben etwas vor zu sein, was sie nicht sind, sie deuten eine logische Beziehung an, die es nicht gibt, weil sich der logische Raum auf die Sprache beschränkt.*)

26. Georges Didi-Huberman, "The Index of the Absent Wound (Monograph on a Stain)," in *OCTOBER; the First Decade* (Cambridge: MIT Press, 1987), 39–57.

27. Ibid., 45.

28. Theodor W. Adorno, *Aesthetic Theory* (London: Routledge & Kegan Paul, 1984), 78.

29. Ibid., 212.

30. Francis Bacon quoted by Giorgio Agamben, *Infancy and History; Essays on the Destruction of Experience* (London: Verso, 1993), 17.

31. Adorno, *Aesthetic Theory*, 55.

32. Ibid., 35–36.

33. See Benjamin's "Surrealism; the Last Snapshot of the European Intelligentsia," in *Reflections* (New York: Schocken Books, 1978), 184.

34. Ludwig Wittgenstein, *Tractatus Logico-Philosophicus* (London: Routledge Kegan Paul, 1990), 183.

35. Martin Heidegger: The Question Concerning Technology," in *Basic Writings* (New York: Harper & Collins, 1993), cf. 337.

36. It comes as no surprise that it was exactly this building task that gathered many of the young architects and architecture students from Graz, who later formed the core of the *Grazer Schule* as members of the design team. Günter Domenig and Eilfried Huth ended up doing a restaurant tower in the Olympia swimming hall; Szyszkowitz and Kowalski, now married, met while working for Behnisch and Otto; Giencke was nearby working for Marete Mattern, the daughter of Hermann Mattern, the landscape architect of Hans Scharoun, who was known for her organic urbanism.

37. Quoted in Kisho Kurokawa, *Metabolism* (Boulder, CO: Westview Press, 1977), 27. Kurokawa extends the concept of *ma* as follows: "Ma has various meanings, amongst them: timing, silence, buffer zone, boundary zone and void. In addition it carries the same connotations as *en*-space or in-between space," 38.

38. Ibid., 33.

39. Ibid., 38.

40. See Buck-Morss, *The Dialectics of Seeing*, 115.

41. Ibid., 125.

42. Lefebvre, *The Production of Space*, 74.

43. The section heading refers to the chapter "How to Make Yourself a Body Without Organs," in Gilles Deleuze and Felix Guattari, *Thousand Plateaus* (Minneapolis: University of Minnesota Press, 1987), 149–166. The following paragraph is relevant to the move I am making, which implies dissolving of the primacy of form and spatial closure: "BwO is made in such a way that it can be occupied, populated only by intensities. Only intensities pass and circulate. . . . The BwO causes intensities to pass, it produces and distributes them in a spatium that is itself intensive, lacking extension. It is not space, nor is it in space; it is matter that occupies space to a given degree—to the degree corresponding to the intensities produced," 153.

44. Jean-Claude Schmitt, "The Ethics of Gesture," in *Fragments for a History of the Human Body*, Michel Feher, Ed. (New York: Zone Books, 1989), 130.

45. Agamben, *Infancy and History*, 140.

46. Gaston Bachelard, *The Poetics of Space* (Boston: Beacon Press, 1958), 222.

47. Lefebvre, *The Production of Space*, 99.

48. Mario Perniola, "Between Clothing and Nudity," in *Fragments for a History of the Human Body* (New York: Zone Books, 1989), 237.

49. Ibid., 242.

50. Ibid., 253.

51. Ibid., 254–255.

52. Similar ideas occur in many other projects by Giencke, including Benedek House, discussed earlier. Several of his unbuilt projects explore the notion even further by putting both structure and material in constant tension, as in *Judohalle* and the carpentry school.

53. Dominique Laporte, *Christo* (New York: Pantheon Books, 1986), 69.

54. Jacques Derrida, "Letter to Peter Eisenman," in *Assemblage* 12 (Cambridge: MIT Press, 1990), 9.

55. Perniola, "Between Clothing and Nudity," pp. 246–248.

Chapter 4

1. Otto Mauer, "Konzept der Rede zur Eröffnung der Galerie St. Stephan," in Robert Fleck, *Avant-Garde in Wien; die Geschichte der Galerie nächst St. Stephan 1954–1982—Kunst und Kunstbetrieb in Österreich (Bank 1: Die Chronik)* (Vienna: Löcker Verlag, 1982), 278 (my translation). ("Yesterday the avant-gardist was destructive, tomorrow he will be affirmative and loving.")

2. Guy Debord, "Preliminary Problems of Constructing Situations," in *Situationist Anthology*, Ken Knabb, Ed. (Berkeley, CA: Bureau of Public Secrets, 1981), 43.

3. Robert Fleck, *Avant-Garde in Wien*, p. 278 (my translation). ("*die Avant-garde, in dem Versuch geeint, das Subjektive (die Innenwelt) zu expandieren, ihr eigenes Tun mit dem Begriff der "Post-Object-Kunst" interpretierend (Ideenkunst, Individuationskunst), zwischen Melancholie und Trauer schwankend.*")

4. Mauer, "Konzept der Rede," 435–436 (my translation). (*Sie [die Kirche] has insofern einen emanzipatorischen Charakter, bleibt aber nicht als "Freiheit von" im Negativen stecken, sondern wendet sich als "Freiheit für" den großen kreativen Aufgaben der Menscheit zu.*)

5. Jacques Derrida, *Writing and Difference* (Chicago: University of Chicago Press, 1978), 234.

6. Henri Lefebvre, *The Production of Space* (Cambridge: Basil Blackwell, 1991), 135.

7. Jochen Schulte-Sasse, Introduction, in Peter Bürger, *Theory of Avant-Garde* (Minneapolis: University of Minnesota Press, 1984), xxvii-xxviii.

8. Ibid., xxix.

9. Bürger, *Theory of Avant-Garde*, 65.

10. Otto Mauer, "Rede über Joseph Beuys," in Fleck, *Avant-Garde in Wien*, 267 (my translation). (*Ich glaube, daß es in der Geschichte der Kunst und in der Weltgeschichte des Geistes sehr lange gedauert hat, bis man sich von allen Klassizismen befreien konnte, von einer Kunst, die kanonischer, das heißt finaler Natur ist, die das darstellt, was sein sollte, nicht das, was ist. Aber dieser Mann, der hier seine Objekte zeigt, ist sozusagen ein Gotiker, ist Realist, kein Klassiker, Ihn interessiert das Faktische, die Existenz. Ihn interessiert nicht die substantia, die natura, die philosophische, die dauernde, für all Zeiten gültige Aussage, die Wesensaussage über die Dinge und über den Menschen, sondern ihn interessiert die Situation; er sagt nichts aus über das "Ewige" im Menschen.*)

11. Ibid., 269 (my translation). (*Sie sind Zeichen für die conditio humana, für unsere zufällige menschliche Existenz.*)

12. See Adorno's discussion of Beethoven in *Aesthetic Theory*, or Schorske's discussion of modulation in *Fin-de-Siècle Vienna*; for both writers the liberation from form correlates with social freedom; inconsistency is a sign of resistance through art.

13. Schulte-Sasse, in Bürger, *Theory of Avant-Garde*, xxxii.

14. See Russell A. Berman's discussion of Austrian postwar politics based on neutrality in chapter 11, "The Vienna Fascination," in *Modern Culture and Critical Theory; Art, Politics, and the Legacy of the Frankfurt School* (Madison: University of Wisconsin Press, 1989), 204–241. Particularly interesting is his discussion on how the discourse fluctuated between the problematics of private versus collective identity.

15. Ibid., 226.

16. Cf. Roland Barthes, *The Barthes Reader*, in Susan Sontag, Ed. (New York: Hill & Wang, 1982), 216.

17. Carl E. Schorske, *Fin-de-Siècle Vienna*, (New York: Vintage Press, 1981), xxiv.

18. Ibid., xxviii.

19. See Günther Domenig, "Gedanken zur Architektur," and Dietmar Steiner, "Helmut Richter—Heidulf Gerngross: Architektur—Zeichen einer Haltung," in *Architektur—Investitionen* (Graz: Akademische Druck- und Verlagsanstalt, 1986), and Volker Giencke, "Du hast nichts anderes als dein Leben . . ." in *Die Brücke 2/91*.

20. Georges Mathieu in an interview with Cathérine Millet (1981), quoted by Fleck, *Avant-Garde in Wien*, 188 (my translation). (*In allen bekannten Gesellschaften wird das Verhalten der Menschen von Glaubenssätzen und Ideologien regiert, welche auf der Erkenntnis von Werten aufbauen, die auf präexistenten Realitäten beruhen. Demgegenüber existiert ertsmals eine Kunst—und sie wird zu einer universellen Sprache—, die jeden Bezug zu einer vorgegebenen Realität durchschnitten hat. Die entscheidende Wende, die sich in der Malerei ereignet hat, erfordert daher—Kunst ist prophetisch—die Umsä^lzung aller entsprechenden Punkte auf dem Gebiet der Ideen und der Sitten. Mit der Lyrischen Abstrak-*)

tion ist nicht nur eine neue Ausdrucksform entstanden, sondern eine neue Weise, der Welt zu begegnen, ausgehend von der radikalen Infragestellung aller unserer abendländischen Dialektiken von Aristoteles bis Derrida! . . . Sobald die Sicherheit besiegt und der Schrecken vorbei ist, werden wir die Verherrlichung des Risikos erleben, dieses Fest des Seins, das nicht nur eine neue Ästhetik eröffnet, sondern eine neue Moral und eine neue Metaphysik.)

21. Günter Brus quoted in Veit Loers, "When Pictures Learnt to Walk," in *Von der Aktionsmalerei zum Aktionismus* (Klagenfurt: Ritter Verlag, 1988), 12.

22. Schulte-Sasse from Bürger, *Theory of Avant-Garde*, xxxi.

23. Friedensreich Hundertwasser, "Mould Manifesto," in Ulrich Conrads, *Programs and Manifestos on 20th-Century Architecture* (Cambridge: MIT Press, 1991), 158–159.

24. Alfons Schilling, in *Von der Aktionsmalerei zum Aktionismus*, 153.

25. Maurice Merleau-Ponty, *The Visible and the Invisible* (Evanston, IL: Northwestern University Press, 1968), 138.

26. Günter Brus, in *Zertrümelte Spiegel; Wiener Aktionismus 1960–1971* (Klagenfurt: Ritter Verlag, 1989), 153. Günter Brus was a leading member of the *Wiener Gruppe* and later of the *Wiener Aktionisten*.

27. Kiesler's importance for the Austrian discourse culminates in two exhibitions: *Galerie nächst St. Stephan* held an exhibition of his work in 1975. A major retrospective of his work is organized in collaboration of the Whitney Museum of American Art in New York and the Museum der Moderner Kunst in Vienna. See exhibition catalog *Friedrich Kiesler—Visionär 1890–1965* (Vienna: Löcker Verlag, 1988).

28. Loers in "When Pictures Learnt to Walk," in *Von der Aktionsmalerei zum Aktionismus*, 19.

29. Theodor W. Adorno, "Looking back on Surrealism," in *Notes to Literature* (New York: Columbia University Press, 1991), Vol. 1, 88.

30. Guy Debord, "Report on the Construction . . ." in *Situationist International Anthology*, Ken Knabb, Ed. (Berkeley, CA: Bureau of Public Secrets, 1981), 22.

31. Ibid., 24.

32. Ibid., 24.

33. Ibid., 25.

34. Raoul Vaneigem quoted by Sadie Plant, *The Most Radical Act* (London: Routledge & Kegan Paul, 1992), 71.

35. Ibid., 22.

36. The avant-garde depends greatly on similar strategy that leads from negation to affirmation and belonging that we find in Turner's description of a rite: "rites of passage or transition are marked in three phases: separation, margin (or limen, signifying 'threshold' in Latin), and aggregation." See Viktor Turner, "Liminality and Community," in *Culture and Society; Contemporary Debates* (Cambridge: Cambridge University Press, 1993), 147–154. Bernice Martin, *A Sociology of Contemporary Cultural Change* (Oxford: Basil Blackwell, 1983) provides an excellent analysis of the relationship between 1960s and 1970s counter-culture, the romantic tradition, and recent social and anthropological theories.

37. Gaston Bachelard, *The Poetics of Space* (Boston: Beacon Press, 1969), 224.

38. Manfredo Tafuri, *Theories and History of Architecture* (New York: Harper & Row, 1980), 104–105.

39. Cf. Jack Zipes's introduction, "Toward a Realization of Anticipatory Illumination," in Ernst Bloch, *The Utopian Function of Art and Literature; Selected Essays,* (Cambridge: MIT Press, 1989).

40. Martin Heidegger, *Being and Time* (New York: Harper & Row, 1962), 176.

41. Ibid., 177.

42. Gilles Deleuze, *Bergsonism* (New York: Zone Books, 1988), 20.

43. Tomás Llorens, Making History, in *Architecture, Criticism, Ideology,* Joan Ockman, Ed. (Princeton: Princeton Architectural Press, 1985), 40.

44. Heidegger, *Being and Time,* 238–239.

45. Ernst Bloch, *The Principle of Hope* (Cambridge: MIT Press, 1986), Vol. 1, 127.

46. Ibid., 221.

47. Gerald L. Bruns, "Poethics: John Cage and Stanley Cavell at the Crossroads of Ethical Theory," in *John Cage Composed in America,* Marjorie Perloff and Charles Junkerman, Ed. (Chicago: University of Chicago Press, 1994), 215–219.

48. Maurice Merleau-Ponty, *The Visible and the Invisible* (Evanston, IL: Northwestern Univ. Press, 1968), 73.

49. Walter Benjamin: "Surrealism; the Last Snapshot of European Intelligentsia," in *Reflections* (New York: Schocken Books, 1978), 180–181.

50. Giorgio Agamben, *Infancy and History,* (London: Verso, 1993), 25–26.

51. Paul Mann: *The Theory-Death of the Avant-Garde* (Indianapolis: Indiana University Press, 1991), 93.

52. Ibid., 93–94.

Bibliography

Philosophy, Aesthetic Theory, and Cultural Criticism

Alexander, Jeffrey C., Ed. *Culture and Society—Contemporary Debates*. Cambridge: Press Syndicate of the University of Cambridge, 1990.

Adorno, Theodor W. *Aesthetic Theory*. Trans. C. Lenhardt, Ed. Gretel Adorno and Rolf Tiedemann. London: Routledge & Kegan Paul, 1984. Originally *Ästhetische Theorie* (Frankfurt: Suhrkamp Verlag, 1970).

Adorno, Theodor W. *Notes to Literature*. Vol. 1, Ed. Rolf Tiedemann, Trans. Shierry Weber Nicholsen. New York: Columbia University Press, 1991. Originally *Noten zur Literatur*. Vol. 1 (Frankfurt: Suhrkamp Verlag, 1958).

Adorno, Theodor W., and Horkheimer, Max. *Dialectic of Enlightenment*. Trans. John Cumming. (New York: Continuum Publication Co., 1972). Originally *Dialektik der Aufklärung* (Frankfurt: Suhrkamp Verlag, 1972).

Agamben, Giorgio. *The Coming Community*. Trans. Michael Hardt. Minneapolis: University of Minnesota Press, 1993. Originally *La Communita che viene* (Turin: Einaudi, 1990).

Agamben, Giorgio. *Infancy and History; Essays on the Destruction of Experience*. Trans. Liz Heron. London: Verso, 1993. Originally *Infanzia e storia* (Turin: Einaudi, 1973).

Agamben, Giorgio. *Stanzas: Word and Phantasm in Western Culture*. Trans. Roland L. Martinez. Minneapolis: University of Minnesota Press, 1993. Originally *Stanze: La parola e il fantasma nella cultura occidentale* (Turin: Einaudi, 1977).

Artaud, Antonin. *Collected Works 2*. Trans. Viktor Corti. London: Calder & Boyars, 1971. Originally *Oeuvres Completes Tome II* (Paris: Editions Gallimard, 1961).

Artaud, Antonin. *Collected Works 4*. Trans. Victor Corti. London: Calder & Boyars, 1974. Originally *Oeuvres Completes Tome IV* (Paris: Editions Gallimard, 1964).

Bachelard, Gaston. *The Poetics of Space*. Trans. Maria Jolas, foreword Etienne Gilson. Boston: Beacon Press, 1969. Originally *La poetique de l'espace* (Paris: Presses Universitaires de France, 1958).

Bachelard, Gaston. *The Right to Dream*. Trans. J. A. Underwood. New York: Grossman Publishers, 1971. Originally *Droit de rêver* (1970).

Bachmayr, Hans Matthäus; Loo, Otto van de; and Rötzer, Florian, Ed. *Bildwelten—Denkbilder*. Munich: Klaus Boer Verlag & Galerie van de Loo, 1986.

Baltrušaitis, Jurgis. *Aberrations: An Essay or the Legend of Forms*. Trans. Richard Miller. Cambridge: MIT Press, 1989. Originally *Aberrations: Essai sur la légende des Formes* (Paris: Flammarion, 1983).

Barthes Roland. *Image, Music, Text*. Trans. Stephen Heath. New York: Farrar, Straus & Giroux, 1988.

Barthes, Roland. *The Pleasure of the Text*. Trans. Richard Miller. New York: Hill & Wang, 1975. Originally *Le Plaisir du texte* (Paris: Editions Gallimard, 1973).

Barthes Roland. *Elements of Semiology*. Trans. Annette Lavers and Colin Smith. New York: Hill & Wang 1968, 1977. Originally *Elements de Semiologie* (Paris: Editions du Seuil, 1964).

Barthes, Roland. *Writing Degree Zero*. Trans. Jonathan Cape. Boston: Beacon Press, 1967. Originally *Le Degré Zéro L'Ecriture* (Paris: Editions du Seuil, 1953).

Benjamin, Walter. *Illuminations*. Trans. Harry Zohn, Ed. Hannah Arendt. New York:

Schocken Books, 1969. Originally *Illuminationen* (Frankfurt: Suhrkamp Verlag, 1955).

Benjamin, Walter. *Reflections: Essays, Aphorisms, Autobiographical Writings.* Trans. Edmund Jephcott, Ed. Peter Demetz. New York: Schocken Books, 1978.

Bergson, Henri. *Matter and Memory.* Trans. Nancy Margaret Paul and W. Scott Palmer. New York: Zone Books, 1988. Originally *Matière et mémoire* (Paris: Felix Alcan, 1896).

Berman, Marshall. *All that Is Solid Melts into Air—The Experience of Modernity.* New York: Penguin Books, 1989.

Berman, Russell A. *Modern Culture and Critical Theory: Art, Politics and the Legacy of the Frankfurt School.* Madison: University of Wisconsin Press, 1989.

Bloch, Ernst. *The Principle of Hope.* Trans. Neville Plaice, Stephen Plaice, and Paul Knight. Cambridge: MIT Press, 1986. Originally *Das Prinzip Hoffnung.* (Frankfurt: Suhrkamp Verlag, 1959.)

Bloch, Ernst. *The Utopian Function of Art and Literature: Selected Essays.* Trans. Jack Zipes and Frank Mecklenburg. Cambridge: MIT Press, 1988.

Brown, Norman O. *Life Against Death; the Psychoanalytical Meaning of History.* Middletown, CT: Wesleyan University Press, 1959.

Buck-Morss, Susan. *The Dialectics of Seeing—Walter Benjamin and the Arcades Project.* Cambridge: MIT Press, 1989.

Bürger, Peter. *Theory of Avant-Garde.* Trans. Michael Shaw, foreword by Jochen Schulte-Sasse. Minneapolis: University of Minnesota Press, 1984. Originally *Theorie der Avantgarde* (Frankfurt: Suhrkamp Verlag, 1974).

Couliano, Ioan O. *Eros and Magic in the Renaissance.* Chicago: University of Chicago Press, 1987. Originally *Eros et magie à la Renaissance* (Paris: Flammarion, 1984).

Deleuze, Gilles. *Bergsonism.* Trans. Hugh Tomlinson. New York: Zone Books, 1988. Originally *Le Bergsonismè* (Paris: Presses Universitaires de France, 1966).

Deleuze, Gilles. *Cinema 1; the Movement-Image.* Trans. Hugh Tomlinson and Barbara Habberjam. London Athlone Press, 1986. Originally *Cinéma 1; Image-Mouvement* (Paris: Editions de Minuit, 1983).

Deleuze, Gilles. *Cinema 2; the Time-Image.* Trans. Hugh Tomlinson and Robert Galeta. Minneapolis: University of Minnesota Press, 1989. Originally *Cinema 2, L'Image-temps* (Paris: Editions de Minuit, 1985).

Deleuze, Gilles. *The Fold, Leibniz and the Baroque.* Trans. Tom Conley. Minneapolis: University of Minnesota Press, 1993. Originally *Le Pli: Leibniz et le baroque* (Paris: Editions de Minuit, 1988).

Deleuze, Gilles, and Felix Guattari. *Anti-Oedipus; Capitalism and Schizophrenia.* Trans. Robert Hurlez, Mark Seem, and Helen R. Lane. New York: Viking Press, 1977. Originally *l'Anti-Oedipe* (Paris: Editions de Minuit, 1972).

Deleuze, Gilles, and Felix Guattari. *Thousand Plateaus.* Trans. Brian Massumi. Minneapolis: University of Minnesota Press, 1987. Originally *Milles Plateaus* (Paris: Editions de Minuit, 1980).

Derrida, Jacques. *Writing and Difference.* Trans. Alan Bass. Chicago: University of Chicago Press, 1978. Originally *L'ecriture et différance* (Paris: Editions du Seuil, 1967).

Feher, Michel, Ed. *Fragments for a History of the Human Body*. New York: Zone Books, 1989.

Foster, Hal, Ed. *Postmodern Culture*. London: Pluto Press, 1985.

Foucault, Michel. "Of Other Spaces," in *Diacritics* (Spring 1986), 22–27. Originally "Des Espaces Autres" (1984).

Freeman, Judi, Ed. *The Dada and Surrealist Word Image*. Cambridge: MIT Press, 1989.

Freud, Sigmund. "Fetishism," in *The Standard Edition of the Complete Works of Sigmund Freud*. Vol. XXI. London: Hogarth Press, 1961.

Focillon, Henri. *The Life of Forms in Art*. Trans. Charles Beecher Hogan and George Kubler. New York: Zone Books, 1989. Originally *La Vie des Formes* (Paris: Presses Universitaires de France, 1934).

Habermas, Jürgen. *The Philosophical Discourse of Modernity: Twelve Lectures*. Trans. Frederick G. Lawrence. Cambridge: MIT Press, 1987. Originally *Der philosophische Diskurs der Moderne: Zwölf Vorlesungen* (Frankfurt: Suhrkamp Verlag, 1985).

Harries, Karsten. "Transformations of the Subjunctive," in *Thought* (September 1980), 283–294.

Harries, Karsten. *The Broken Frame*. Washington, DC. Catholic University Press, 1989.

Harvey, David. *The Condition of Postmodernity*. Cambridge: Blackwell Publishers, 1989.

Heidegger, Martin. *Basic Writings*. Ed. David Farrell Krell. New York: HarperCollins, 1977.

Heidegger, Martin. *Being and Time*. Trans. John Macquarrie and Edward Robinson. New York: Harper & Row, 1962. Originally *Sein und Zeit* (Tübingen: Neomarius Verlag, 1927).

Heidegger, Martin. *On the Way to Language*. Trans. Peter D. Hertz. New York: Harper & Row, 1971. Originally *Unterwegs zur Sprache* (Pfullingen: Verlag Günther Neske, 1959).

Heidegger, Martin. *Poetry, Language, Thought*. Trans. Albert Hofstadter. New York: Harper & Row, 1975.

Heidegger, Martin. *The Question Concerning Technology and Other Essays*. Trans. and introduction by William Lovits. New York: Garland Publishing, 1977.

Jameson, Fredric. *The Political Unconscious; Narrative as a Socially Symbolic Act*. Ithaca, NY: Cornell University Press, 1981.

Kristeva, Julia. *Desire in Language*. New York: Columbia University Press, 1982.

Kristeva, Julia. *Revolution in Poetic Language*. Trans. Margaret Waller, introduction by Leon S. Roudiez. New York: Columbia University Press, 1984. Originally *La revolution du langage poetique* (Paris: Editions du Seuil, 1974).

Lefebvre, Henri. *Critique of Everyday Life*. Vol. I. Introduction. Trans. John Moore, preface by Michel Trebitsch. London: Verso, 1991. Originally *Critique de la vie quotidienne. I. Introduction* (Paris: Editions Grasset, 1947).

Lefebvre, Henri. *The Production of Space*. Trans. Donald Nicholson-Smith. Cambridge: Basil Blackwell, 1991. Originally *La Production de l'espace* (Paris: Editions Antropos, 1974).

Lyotard, Jean Paul. *The Inhuman; Reflections on Time*. Trans. Geoffrey Bennington and Rachel Bowlby. Stanford, CA: Stanford University Press, 1991. Originally *L'inhumain: Causeries sur le Temps* (Paris: Editions Galilee, 1988).

Mann, Paul. *The Theory-Death of the Avant-Garde*. Bloomington: Indiana University Press, 1991.

Marcuse, Herbert. *Eros and Civilization*. Boston: Beacon Press, 1955.

Marcuse, Herbert. *The One-Dimensional Man: Studies in the Ideology of Advanced Industrial Society*. Boston: Beacon Press, 1964.

Martin, Bernice. *A Sociology of Contemporary Cultural Change*. Oxford: Basil Blackwell, 1981.

McFarlane, James. "The Mind of Modernism," in *Modernism*. Ed. Malcolm Bradbury and James McFarlane. London: Penguin Books, 1976.

Merleau-Ponty, Maurice. *Phenomenology of Perception*. Trans. Colin Smith. New York: Routledge & Kegan Paul, 1962. Originally *Phenomenologie de la Perception* (Paris: Editions Gallimard, 1945).

Merleau-Ponty, Maurice. *The Visible and the Invisible*. Trans. Alphonso Lingis, Ed. Claude Lefort. Evanston, IL: Northwestern University Press, 1968. Originally *Le Visible et l'invisible* (Paris: Editions Gallimard, 1964).

Nancy, Jean-Luc. *The Experience of Freedom*. Trans. Bridget McDonald. Stanford, CA: Stanford University Press, 1993. Originally *L'Experience de la liberté* (Paris: Editions Galilee, 1988).

Nietzsche, Friedrich. *The Birth of Tragedy and the Case of Wagner*. Trans. Walter Kaufmann. New York: Random House, 1967.

Poggioli, Renato. *The Theory of the Avant-Garde*. Trans. Gerald Fitzgerald. Cambridge: Harvard University Press, 1968. Originally *Theoria dell'arte d'avantguardia* (Milan: Societa editrice il Mulino, 1962).

Poster, Mark. *Existential Marxism in Postwar France; from Sartre to Althusser*. Princeton: Princeton University Press, 1975.

Prange, Regine. *Das Kristalline als Kunstsymbol—Bruno Taut und Paul Klee*. Hildesheim: Georg Olms Verlag, 1991.

Ricouer, Paul. "The Problem of Double-Sense as Hermeneutic Problem and as Semantic Problem," in *Myths and Symbols: Studies in Honor of Mircea Eliade*. Ed. Joseph M. Kitagawa and Charles H. Long. Chicago: University of Chicago Press, 1969.

Rorty, Richard. *Philosophy and the Mirror of Nature*. Princeton: Princeton University Press, 1979.

Sartre, Jean Paul. *Being and Nothingness; an Essay on Phenomenal Ontology*. Trans. Hazel E. Barnes. New York: Philosophical Library, 1956. Originally *L'être et le néant; essai d'ontologie phénoménologique* (Paris: Editions Gallimard, 1943).

Scarry, Elaine. *The Body in Pain: The Making and Unmaking of the World*. Oxford: Oxford University Press, 1985.

Schiller, Johann. *On the Aesthetic Education of Man, in a Series of Letters*. Oxford: Clarendon Press, 1982. Originally *Über die ästhetische Erziehung des Menschen in einer Reihe von Briefen* (Frankfurt: Suhrkamp Verlag, 1984).

Sedlmayr, Hans. *Art in Crisis, the Lost Center*. Chicago: Henry Cegnery Company, 1958. Originally *Verlust der Mitte* (Salzburg: Otto Müller Verlag, 1948).

Simmel, Georg. "Metropolis and Mental Life," in *Georg Simmel, On Individuality and Social Forms*. Trans. and Ed. Donald Levine. Chicago: University of Chicago Press, 1985.

Sontag, Susan, Ed. and foreword. *A Barthes Reader*. New York: Hill & Wang, 1982.

Virilio, Paul. *The Aesthetics of Disappearance*. Trans. Philip Beitchman. New York: Semiotext(e), 1991. Originally *Estetique de la disparition* (Paris: Editions Balland, 1980).

Virilio, Paul. *The Lost Dimension.* Trans. Daniel Moshenberg. New York: Semiotext(e),
    1991. Originally *L'espace critique* (Paris: Christian Bourgois, 1984).

Wittgenstein, Ludwig. *Tractacus Logico-Philosophicus.* London: Routledge & Kegan Paul,
    1922.

Žižek, Slavoj. *Looking Awry: An Introduction to Jacques Lacan through Popular Culture.* Cambridge: MIT
    Press, 1991.

Yates, Frances. *The Art of Memory.* London: Routledge & Kegan Paul, 1966.

Architectural Criticism

Adorno, Theodor W. "Functionalism Today," in *Oppositions* 17 (New York: Institute for
    Architecture and Urban Studies, 1977), 31–53.

Banham, Reyner. *Design by Choice.* Ed. Penny Sparke. New York: Rizzoli, 1981.

Banham, Reyner. *Theory and Design in the First Machine Age.* London: Architectural Press,
    1960.

Banham, Reyner. *Megastructure, Urban Futures of the Recent Past.* New York: Harper & Row,
    1979.

Behrens, Peter. "On Art of the Stage," in *Perspecta* 26. Trans. Howard Fitzpatrick. (New
    Haven: New York: Perspecta Incorporated and Rizzoli, 1990). Originally "Über
    die Kunst auf der Bühne" (Frankfurter Zeitung, 1910.)

Blundell-Jones, Peter. *Hans Scharoun; a Monograph.* London: Gordon Fraser, 1978.

Cacciari, Massimo. *Architecture of Nihilism, on the Philosophy of Modern Architecture.* Trans. Patrizia
    Lombardo. New Haven: Yale University Press, 1993.

Connah, Roger. *Writing Architecture: Fantômas, Fragments, Fictions: An Architectural Journey through
    the 20th Century.* Cambridge: MIT Press, 1989.

Conrads, Ulrich. *Programs and Manifestoes on 20th-Century Architecture.* Trans. Michael Bullock.
    Cambridge: MIT Press, 1971.

Cook, Peter. *New Spirit in Architecture.* New York: Rizzoli, 1991.

Dal Co, Fransesco. *Figures of Architecture and Thought; German Architectural Culture 1880–1920.*
    New York: Rizzoli 1990.

Derrida, Jacques. "Letter to Peter Eisenman," in *Assemblage* 12 (Cambridge: MIT Press,
    1990).

Giedion, Siegfried. *Space, Time and Architecture.* Cambridge: Harvard University Press,
    1954.

Frampton, Kenneth. *Modern Architecture; a Critical History.* New York: Thames & Hudson,
    1992.

Harries, Karsten. *The Baroque Rococo Church: Between Faith and Aestheticism.* New Haven: Yale
    University Press, 1983.

Harries, Karsten. "Theatricality and Re-presentation; Nineteenth Century Culture, Its
    Architecture and Theater Architecture," in *Perspecta* 26 (New Haven and New York:
    Perspecta Incorporated and Rizzoli, 1990).

Hays, Michael. *Modernism and the Posthumanist Subject—the Architecture of Hannes Mayer and Ludwig
    Hilbersheimer.* Cambridge: MIT Press, 1992.

Joedicke, Jürgen. *Moderne Architektur: Strömungen und Tendenzen.* Stuttgart: Karl Krämer, 1969.

Kurokawa, Kisho. *Metabolism*. Boulder, CO: Westview Press, 1977.

Le Corbusier. *Towards a New Architecture*. New York: Holt, Rinehard & Winston, 1960. Originally *Vers Une Architecture* (Paris: Editions Crès, 1923).

Müller, Michael. *Die Verdrängung des Ornaments; Zum Verhältnis von Architektur und Lebenspraxis.* Frankfurt: Suhrkamp Verlag, 1977.

Noever, Peter, Ed. *Architecture in Transition; Between Deconstruction and New Modernism*. Munich: Prestel, 1991.

Ockman, Joan, Ed. *Architecture, Criticism, Ideology*. Princeton: Princeton Architectural Press, 1985.

Ockman, Joan, and Eigen, Edward, Ed. *Architecture Culture 1943–1968; a Documentary Anthology*. New York: Columbia Books of Architecture and Rizzoli, 1993.

Porphyriou, Dimitri. *Modern Eclectism*. London: Academy Editions, 1982.

Rowe, Colin. *The Mathematics of the Ideal Villa and Other Essays*. Cambridge: MIT Press, 1976.

Scheerbart, Paul. *Glass Architecture*. Trans. James Palmes, Ed. Dennis Sharp. New York: Praeger Publishers, 1972.

Taut, Bruno. *Alpine Architecture*. Trans. Shirley Palmer, Ed. Dennis Sharp. New York: Praeger Publishers, 1972.

Whyte, Ian Boyd. *Bruno Taut and the Architecture of Activism*. New York: Cambridge University Press, 1982.

Whyte, Iain Boyd. *The Crystal Chain Letters, Architectural Fantasies by Bruno Taut and His Circle*. Cambridge: MIT Press, 1985.

Vidler, Anthony. "The Explosion of Space: Architecture and the Filmic Imaginary," in *Assemblage 21*.

Wines, James. *De-Architecture*. New York: Rizzoli, 1987.

Zevi, Bruno. *Towards Organic Architecture*. London: Faber & Faber, 1949.

Austria: Art and Architecture

Achleitner, Friedrich. *Neue Architektur in Österreich 1945–1970*. Vienna: Österreichische Fachzeitschriften, 1969.

Achleitner, Friedrich. *Österreichische Architektur im 20. Jahrhundert; Ein Führer in drei Bänden*. Vienna: Residenz Verlag, 1989.

Anderson, Mark. "The Ornaments of Writing: Kafka, Loos and the Jugendstil," in *New German Critique* (Winter 1988), 125–145.

"Austrian Ambivalence," *Architectural Review* no. 1102 (December 1988).

"Autriche, Vienna et Graz," *l'Architecture d'Ajourd'hui* no. 264 (September 1986).

Bogner, Dieter. *Friedrich Kiesler; Architekt, Maler, Bildhauer 1890–1965*. Vienna: Löcker Verlag, 1988.

Brückner, Günter. *Barockarchitektur in Österreich*. Cologne: DuMont, 1983.

Colomina, Beatriz. *Raumplan versus Plan Libre*. New York: Rizzoli, 1991.

Comini, Alessandra. *Fantastic Art of Vienna*. New York: Knopf, 1.978.

Comini, Alessandra. "Intimacy and Spectacle; the Interiors of Adolf Loos," in *AA files* 10 (Autumn 1985).

COOP Himmelblau. *Architecture Is Now; Projects, (Un)buildings, Actions, Statements, Sketches, Commentaries 1968–1983*. New York: Rizzoli, 1983.

Dimster, Frank. *New Austrian Architecture*. New York: Rizzoli, 1988.

Feuerstein, Günter. *Visionäre Architektur Wien 1958–88*. Berlin: Ernst & Sohn, 1988.

Fleck, Robert. *Avant-Garde in Wien: Die Geschichte der Galerie nächst St. Stephan Wien 1954–1982; Kunst und Kunstbetrieb in Österreich*. Vienna: Löcker Verlag, 1982.

Gieselbrecht, Ernst, et al. *Architektur aus Graz*. Graz: Zentralvereinigung der Architekten, Landesverband Steiermark 1981.

Graf, Otto Antonia. "Wagner and the Vienna School," in *The Anti-Rationalists*. Ed. J. M. Richards and Nicolaus Persner. London: Architectural Press, 1973.

Hellmayr, Nikolaus, Ed. *Architektur als Engagement; Architektur aus der Steiermark 1986–1992*. Graz: Haus der Architektur, 1992.

Hollein, Hans. *MANtransFORMS; Konzepte einer Ausstellung*. Vienna: Löcker Verlag, 1989.

Kapfinger, Otto and Kneissl, Franz E. *Dichte Packung; Architektur aus Wien*. Vienna: Residenz Verlag, 1989.

Klocker, Hubert, Ed. *Der Zertrümelte Spiegel; Wiener Aktionismus 1960–1971*. Klagenfurt: Ritter Verlag, 1989.

Klotz, Heinrich. *Haus-Rucker-Co 1967 bis 1983*. Braunschweig: Friedrich Vieweg & Sohn, 1984.

Kolbowki, Sylvia, Ed. *Austrian New Wave*. New York: IAUS, 1980.

Loos, Adolf. *Spoken into the Void; Collected Essays 1897–1900*. Trans. Jane O. Newman and John H. Smith. Cambridge: MIT Press, 1982. Originally *Ins Leere gesprochen* (Vienna and Munich: Herold, 1962).

Mallgrave, Harry Francis. *Otto Wagner; Reflections on the Raiment of Modernity*. Santa Monica, CA: Getty Center, 1993.

"The New Spirit," in *Architectural Review* no. 1074 (August 1986).

Noever, Peter, Ed. *Günther Domenig: Das Steinhaus*. Klagenfurt: Ritter Verlag, 1989.

Oberhuber, Oswald. *Österreichische Avant-garde 1900–1938: ein unbekannter Aspekt*. Vienna: Galerie nächst St. Stephan, 1976.

Plischke, Ernst A. *Ein Leben mit Architektur*. Vienna: Löcker Verlag, 1989.

Pogöschnik, Ernst, Ed. *Schule und Architektur*. Graz: Steiermärkische Landesdruckerei, 1994.

"Responsive Irregularity," *Architectural Review* no. 1140 (February 1992).

Safran, Yehuda. "Curvature of the Spine: Krauss, Loos and Wittgenstein," in *9H* no. 4 (1983).

Schorske, Carl L. *Fin-de-Siecle Vienna*. New York: Vintage Books, 1961.

Schwartz, Dieter, and Loers, Veit, eds. *Von der Aktionsmalerei Zum Aktionismus 1960–1965*. Klagenfurt: Ritter Verlag, 1988.

Sedlmayr, Hans. *Österreichische Barockarchitektur 1690–1740*. Vienna: Dr. Benno Filser, 1930.

Spalt, Johannes, and Czeck, Hermann. *Josef Frank 1885–1967*. Vienna: Löcker Verlag, 1989.

Steiner, Dietmar, Ed. *Architektur—Investitionen: Grazer "Schule" 13 Standpunkte*. Graz: Akademische Druck- und Verlagsanstalt, 1986.

Sucher, Charlotte. *20 Jahre steirischer herbst 1968–1987.* Vienna: Paul Zsolhay Verlag, 1988.

Szyszkowitz, Michael et al., Ed. *Architektur aus Graz—Öffentliche Bauten und Projekte von 1980 bis heute.* Brussels: Centre d'Information de l'Architecture, de l'Urbanisme et du Design, 1987.

Weibel, Peter, and Christa Steinle. *Identität—Differenz; Tribune Trigon 1940–1990—Eine Topographie der Moderne.* Vienna, Cologne, and Weimar: Böhlau Verlag, 1992.

Wohnbau in Steiermark 1980–1986. Graz: Zentralvereinigung der Architekten, Landesverband Steiermark, 1986.

Wohnbau in Steiermark 1986–1993. Graz: Zentralvereinigung der Architekten, Landesverband Steiermark, 1993.

Zinganel, Peter, ed. *Standpunkte '94* (Graz: Forum Stadtpark, 1994).

Art, Artists, and Art Criticism

Barthes, Roland. "Non Multa Sed Multum," ed. Yuon Lambert in *Cataloque Raisonne des oeuvres sur papier de Cy Twombly* (Milan: Multhipla 1977).

Godard, Jean-Luc. *Godard on Godard.* Trans. Martin Secker. New York: Viking Press, 1972. Originally *Jean-Luc Godard par Jean-Luc Godard* (Paris: Pierre Belfond, 1968).

Holt, Nancy, Ed. *The Writings of Robert Smithson.* New York: New York University Press, 1979.

Jacob, Mary Jane. *Cordon Matta-Clark, Retrospective.* Chicago: Museum of Contemporary Art, 1985.

Knabb, Ken. *Situationist Anthology.* Berkeley, CA: Bureau of Public Secrets, 1981.

Krauss, Rosalin. *The Originality of Avant-Garde and Other Modernist Myths.* Cambridge: MIT Press, 1985.

Krauss, Rosalin. *Passages in Modern Sculpture.* Cambridge: MIT Press, 1981.

Laporte, Dominique. *Christo.* Trans. Abby Pollak. New York: Pantheon Books, 1986.

Malsch, Friedeman. "Gordon Matta-Clark," in *Kunstforum* no. 117 (1992).

Michelson, Annette; Krauss, Rosalin; Grimp, Douglas; and Copjec, Joan, Ed. *OCTOBER; the First Decade.* Cambridge: MIT Press, 1987.

Owens, Craig. "Earthwords," in *October* 16 (Fall 1984).

Paz, Octavio. *Marcel Duchamp, Appearance Stripped Bare.* Trans. Rachel Phillips and Donald Gardner. New York: Viking Press, 1978.

Perloff, Marjorie and Junkerman, Charles. *John Cage Composed in America.* Chicago: University of Chicago Press, 1994.

Pelzer, Birgit. "Vision in Process," in *October* 10 (Fall 1979).

Owens, Craig. "The Allegorical Impulse," in *October* 12 (Spring 1980).

Plant, Sadie. *The Most Radical Act—The Situationist International in a Postmodern Age.* London: Routledge & Kegan Paul, 1992.

Sussman, Elisabeth, ed. *On the Passage of a Few People Through a Rather Brief Moment in Time: The Situationist International 1957–1972.* Cambridge: MIT Press, 1989.

Sylvester, David. *The Brutality of Fact: Interviews with Francis Bacon.* London: Thames & Hudson, 1975.

Wenders, Wim, and Handke, Peter. *Der Himmel über Berlin: ein Filmbuch.* Frankfurt: Suhrkamp Verlag, 1989.

Illustration Credits

Akademie der Künste, Sammlung Baukunst, Berlin: figs. 2.35, 2.36, 2.37, 2.53

Copyright Fratelli Alinari, Florence: figs. 3.56, 3.57

Copyright 1994 The Art Institute of Chicago, Chicago: fig. 3.5

Copyright 1994 The Art Institute of Chicago, Chicago, gift of Winslow Brothers: fig. 3.3

Copyright Estate Francis Bacon, courtesy Marlborough Fine Art Ltd., London: fig. 2.7

Copyright Estate Joseph Beuys/1995 ARS, New York/VG Bild-Kunst, Bonn, collection of Walker Art Center, Minneapolis, gift of John Stoller 1995: fig. 4.2

Copyright cliche Bibliotheque Nationale de France, Paris: figs. 2.22, 3.35

Bildarchiv der Österreichischen Nationalbibliothek, Vienna: figs. 3.21, 4.5, 4.6

Bundesdenkmalamt, Vienna: figs. 3.22, 4.11

Deutsches Architektur-Museum, Frankfurt a.M.: fig. 2.50

Courtesy DIA-Center for the Arts, New York: fig. 4.33

Reproduced from Gunther Feuerstein, *Visionare-Architektur Wien 1958–1988* (Berlin: Ernst & Sohn, 1988): figs. 4.13, 4.27

Copyright Fondation Jean Dubuffet/1995 ARS, New York/ADAGP, Paris: figs. 4.16, 4.17

Courtesy of Galerie Ulysses, Vienna: figs. 4.8, 4.22

Getty Center Resource Collection, Santa Monica: fig. 4.35

Collection of Haags Gemeentemuseum, der Haag: fig. 2.17, 4.21, 4.30

Copyright Harel, Vienna: figs. 4.14, 4.15

Reproduced from Pontus Hulten, *Jean Tinguely: A Magic Stronger than Death* (New York: Abbeville Press, 1987): fig. 3.37

Copyright Estate Frederick Kiesler, courtesy of Jason McCoy Inc., New York, collection of Mrs. Isobel Grossman: fig. 1.13

Courtesy of Mrs. Lillian Kiesler, collection of Whitney Museum of American Art, New York, gift of Mrs. Lillian Kiesler: fig. 4.25

Reproduced from Hubert Klocker (ed.), *Der Zerstrumelte Spiegel: Wiener Aktionismus 1960–1971* (Klagenfurt: Ritter Verlag, 1989): figs. 4.9, 4.10, 4.29

Landesmuseum Joanneum, Bild- und Tonarchiv, Graz: figs. 1.2, 1.17, 3.23, 3.24, 4.4

Reproduced from *Macdonald and Salter Building Projects 1982–1986* (London: Architectural Association, 1987): fig. 3.55

Copyright Estate Gordon Matta-Clark, courtesy of Holly Salomon Gallery, New York: fig. 2.23

Museum of Finnish Architecture, Helsinki: figs. 1.3, 1.14, 2.45, 2.47

Copyright The Museum of Modern Art, New York, advisory comittee fund: fig. 3.36

Copyright The Museum of Modern Art, New York, gift of the architect: figs. 1.15, 1.16, 2.51

Reproduced from *Jean Prouve: Architecture /Industrie* (Paris: Klient, 1989): figs. 3.41, 3.50

Copyright Royal Institute of British Architects, courtesy British Architectural Library/RIBA, London: fig. 2.21

Reproduced from Dieter Schwarz, Veit Loers (eds.), *Von der Aktionsmalerei zum Aktionismus 1960–65* (Klagenfurt: Ritter Verlag, 1988): fig. 3.1

Staatsgalerie Stuttgart. Graphische Sammlung: fig. 2.52

Trinity College Library, manuscript department, Dublin: fig. 3.4

Reproduced from Konrad Wachsmann, *Wendepunkt im Bauen* (Wiesbaden: Krausskopf, 1959): fig. 3.51

Copyright 1995 Whitney Museum of American Art, New York, collection of Whitney Museum of American Art, gift of Mrs. Lillian Kiesler: fig. 4.24

Index

Numerals in italic indicate figures.